THE ROVER BOYS
ON A HUNT

OR, THE MYSTERIOUS HOUSE IN THE WOODS

ARTHUR M. WINFIELD

(Edward Stratemeyer)

1ˢᵗ WORLD
LIBRARY
Literary Society

The Rover Boys on a Hunt

Arthur M. Winfield

© 1st World Library, 2009
PO Box 2211
Fairfield, IA 52556
www.1stworldlibrary.com
First Edition

LCCN: 2009923368

Softcover ISBN: 978-1-4218-8815-6
Hardcover ISBN: 978-1-4218-8914-6
eBook ISBN: 978-1-4218-8716-6

Purchase *"The Rover Boys on a Hunt"*
as a traditional bound book at:
www.1stWorldLibrary.com/purchase.asp?ISBN=978-1-4218-8815-6

1st World Library is a literary, educational organization
dedicated to:

- Creating a free internet library of downloadable ebooks

- Hosting writing competitions and offering book publishing
scholarships.

Interested in more 1st World Library books? contact:
literacy@1stworldlibrary.com
Check us out at: www.1stworldlibrary.com

1st World Library Literary Society

Giving Back to the World

"If you want to work on the core problem, it's early school literacy."

- James Barksdale, former CEO of Netscape

"No skill is more crucial to the future of a child, or to a democratic and prosperous society, than literacy."

- Los Angeles Times

"Literacy... means far more than learning how to read and write... The aim is to transmit... knowledge and promote social participation."

- UNESCO

"Literacy is not a luxury, it is a right and a responsibility. If our world is to meet the challenges of the twenty-first century we must harness the energy and creativity of all our citizens."

- President Bill Clinton

"Parents should be encouraged to read to their children, and teachers should be equipped with all available techniques for teaching literacy, so the varying needs and capacities of individual kids can be taken into account."

- Hugh Mackay

CONTENTS

INTRODUCTION

MY DEAR BOYS: This book is a complete story in itself, but forms the fourth volume in a line issued under the general title, "The Second Rover Boys Series for Young Americans."

As mentioned in some volumes of the first series, this line was started years ago with the publication of "The Rover Boys at School," "On the Ocean," and "In the Jungle," in which I introduced my readers to Dick, Tom and Sam Rover. The twenty volumes of the first series related the doings of these three youths while attending Putnam Hall Military Academy, Brill College, and while on numerous outings.

Having acquired a thorough education, the three young men established themselves in business and were married. Presently Dick Rover became the father of a son and a daughter, and so did his brother Sam, while Tom Rover became the father of twin boys. The four lads were later on sent to boarding school, as related in the first volume of this second series, entitled "The Rover Boys at Colby Hall."

From Colby Hall the scene was shifted to "Snowshoe Island," where the lads went for a winter outing. Then they came back to the military academy, and later on participated in the annual encampment, as related in the third volume, entitled "The Rover Boys under Canvas."

In the present volume the scene is shifted from lively times at Colby Hall to still more livelier times in the woods, to which the lads journeyed for a season of hunting. They came upon a mysterious house in the forest, and there uncovered a secret which I will leave the pages that follow to relate.

Once more I wish to thank my numerous readers for the many nice things they have said about these "Rover Boys" books. I trust that the reading of the volumes will do them all good.

Affectionately and sincerely yours,

EDWARD STRATEMEYER.

Arthur M. Winfield

CHAPTER I

THE BOBSLED RACE

"All ready, boys?"

"Wait a minute, Jack."

"Can't wait; life is too short!" cried Jack Rover gayly. He was seated at the front of a long bobsled holding six boys. "Remember, we've got to be back at the Hall in half an hour."

"Please don't mention it!" pleaded Randy Rover, his cousin.

"Hi, you fellows! are you going to race or not?" came from another youth on a bobsled standing close by.

"You bet we're going to race!" sang out Fred Rover, who was at the tail end of the first sled. "And we'll beat you, too, Bill Glutts!"

"You will, like fun!" grumbled the cadet addressed, a rather heavy-set and by-no-means pre-possessing youth. "Come on now, unless you're afraid."

"We're afraid of nobody!" sang out Andy Rover, and, leaning

sideways from where he sat on the bobsled, he scooped up a handful of loose snow and threw it playfully at Glutts.

"Hi, you! what do you mean?" roared Bill Glutts in anger, as the snow landed directly behind his right ear.

"Hello! I guess it must have begun to snow again," cried Randy Rover, mischievously.

"I'll 'snow' you!" retorted Glutts. "I guess you fellows are afraid to race. That's why you are cutting up."

"Never mind—race them anyway, Bill," came from a small, pasty-faced youth, who was usually called Codfish on account of his broad mouth. "Go ahead and show 'em what your new bobsled can do."

"That's the talk!" cried another cadet, a newcomer at the academy. "Show 'em that the *Yellow Streak* can lick anything on this hill."

"That's a dream that will never come true!" cried Spouter Powell. "Come ahead, Jack, let's start this race," he added to the oldest Rover boy.

The scene was Long Hill, a rise of ground located about midway between Colby Hall Military Academy and the town of Haven Point. There was something of a wagon road leading up the hill from the main highway which skirted Clearwater Lake, and this road had been converted by the cadets of the academy into a slide for their bobsleds.

From the top of the hill the slide ran down and over two smaller hills, then crossed the main highway and shot down another road onto the lake, which at this season of the year was covered with ice.

Arthur M. Winfield

It was a Saturday afternoon, and, as usual, the cadets of the military academy were making the most of their off time, some with bobsleds and other with ordinary handsleds and what were locally called "bread shovels."

For some weeks before this the boys, as well as many other residents in that vicinity, had enjoyed skating on the lake. But a rather wet snow had fallen which the wind had been unable to sweep away, and consequently skating became a thing of the past. Then the lads turned to their bobsleds, the Rovers getting out one they had used the season before. This they painted and varnished very carefully and christened the *Blue Moon*.

"Because, you see," explained Randy, with a wink, "it's only once in a blue moon that she'll be beaten."

The Rovers and their chums, as well as many other cadets and boys and girls from that vicinity, had been using the hill for a couple of hours when the race between the *Blue Moon* and the *Yellow Streak* was proposed by Nick Carncross, the new friend of Bill Glutts.

Now, as my old readers know, the Rovers and Bill Glutts were by no means on good terms with each other. In the past Glutts had proved himself anything but a friend, and they had had more than one personal encounter with this freckled-faced bully.

But it was not in the nature of any of the Rover boys to refuse a challenge to race, knowing well that if this was done many would think they were afraid of being beaten. So the challenge was accepted, and immediately the details were arranged.

Each bobsled was to carry six cadets, and they were to start down the hill side by side, the *Blue Moon* keeping well to the right and the *Yellow Streak* well to the left. The first sled to cross a mark located out on the lake was to be declared the winner.

With the four Rover boys were their intimate chums, Spouter Powell and Gif Garrison. With Glutts were Codfish, Carncross, and three other of the bully's cronies.

"Gee! I wish I was in that race," came from Will Hendry, who, on account of his unusual stoutness, was always called Fatty.

"Nothing doing, Fatty," remarked Dan Soppinger, another cadet. "You'd make the Rovers lose sure."

"All ready?" questioned Walt Baxter, who had been settled on as the starter of the race.

"All ready," answered Jack Rover, after a glance around to see that nothing was out of order.

"Been ready half an hour," grumbled Bill Glutts.

"All right, then!" cried Walt. "One—two—three—go!"

As he finished Fred Rover, who was at the rear of the *Blue Moon*, gave that bobsled a quick push and leaped aboard. At the same time Carncross sent the *Yellow Streak* forward and also sprang to his seat. Then, side by side, the two bobsleds moved down the long hill, slowly at first, but gradually gathering speed.

It was five o'clock of an afternoon in early December, and consequently quite dark, even on the snow-clad hills. Many of the smaller children, and also the girls, had gone home, leaving the place to the cadets and a few others.

"I hope we win this," remarked Randy, as the two sleds continued to speed forward side by side.

"Of course we'll win it," came promptly from Gif Garrison.

"We've got to win it!" added Fred Rover.

"If you don't win Bill Glutts will never stop crowing over you," put in Spouter Powell.

"Hi, there, Glutts! Keep to your side of the run," warned Jack suddenly. The *Yellow Streak* had swerved over well into the middle of the road.

"I know what I'm doing," growled Glutts. "You tend to your own business."

"Well, you know the rules," warned Jack. "You keep over on your own side. If you don't there'll be trouble."

"Humph! you don't have to tell me what to do," growled the other cadet; and then, striking a bit of extra smooth roadway, the *Yellow Streak* bounded ahead, much to the delight of its riders.

"Hurrah! here is where we leave them behind," sang out Codfish.

"Nothing to it but the shouting," added another of Bill Glutts' cronies.

"We'll be a mile ahead by the time we reach the lake," exulted Nick Carncross.

For half a minute it looked as if his prophecy might be true. The *Yellow Streak* was gliding over the icy surface of the long hill, and consequently going ahead, while the *Blue Moon* struck several soft spots where going was anything but good.

"Oh, Jack! can't you pull out of this?" queried Gif Garrison anxiously. "Pull over to the left where the going is harder. It's too soft here entirely."

"I'm sticking to my side of the road, just as I was expected to do," said Jack grimly.

The *Yellow Streak* disappeared over the first rise, and for a few seconds was lost to view. But then the *Blue Moon* came along, and beyond this rise found going somewhat easier. Slowly but surely they crawled up behind the other bobsled.

"Keep to your side of the road, Glutts!" yelled Jack, in a second warning. "If you don't, there'll be trouble."

"And you'll get the worst of it," added Randy.

"I know what I'm doing," retorted Glutts. He had found the snow somewhat soft on his side of the road, and was now running near the center, and occasionally crowding to Jack's side.

"We'll run into 'em sure!" came from Spouter Powell in alarm. "Look out, Jack!"

"Look out!" echoed Fred.

"Over on your own side, or we'll smash you, Glutts!" yelled Jack, for the *Blue Moon* had suddenly found going much easier and was forging forward rapidly. "Get out of the way!"

The call was so peremptory that Glutts felt bound to obey. He swerved to his side of the road, and with not a second to spare, for almost instantly the *Blue Moon* shot past and continued down the slope toward the lake.

"We win! we win!" yelled Andy gayly.

"But the *Yellow Streak* is just behind us!" cried Spouter, looking back. "Here they come!"

"Yes, and on our side of the road, too!" cried Fred, in alarm. He turned his head still further around. "Glutts, get to your own side!"

"Aw, dry up!" cried the other cadet, in disgust. "You don't have to act as if you owned the whole road."

"You know the rules of the race," flung back Fred.

Crossing the highway which skirted the lake was not so easy, and beyond this the snow was rather deep, and consequently the speed of the *Blue Moon* was slackened. The *Yellow Streak* came dangerously close, and then Bill Glutts seemed to lose his head completely. He slued around to his own side of the road, but made such a short turn that in a twinkling the long bobsled was upset and the occupants hurled in all directions.

"There they go! They are upset!" yelled Fred. And then he lost sight of those left behind as the *Blue Moon* shot out on the surface of the lake and beyond the mark set for the end of the race.

"We win! we win!" cried Andy, leaping from the bobsled, and in the exuberance of his spirits he turned a handspring in the snow.

"What happened to the other sled?" asked Jack, who had been so busy steering the *Blue Moon* he had paid little attention to what had been going on behind.

"They had a spill," answered Fred. "But before they took it they came pretty close to running into us."

"It was up to them to keep to their side of the road," said Gif Garrison. "Why, we might have had a terrible accident if they had run into us!"

There were about a dozen boys on the lake who had witnessed the finish of the race, and these, along with those who had come down on the *Blue Moon*, now turned back to see what had happened to the Glutts party. They found the cadets who had been spilled picking themselves up and brushing the snow from their garments. One was nursing a bruised ankle, and another a bruised elbow, while Bill Glutts was wiping some blood from a scratch on his chin.

"Well, we won the race," said Jack briefly. He had no desire to crow over his opponents.

"Huh! you didn't win it fairly," growled Glutts, glaring at him.

"Didn't win it fairly!" exclaimed Jack. "What do you mean by that?"

"I mean you got in our way so we couldn't get past you— that's what I mean!" growled the other.

"That is false, Glutts, and you know it," retorted the oldest Rover boy.

"See here, Jack Rover! you can't talk to me in that fashion," roared Bill Glutts. He had been in a more or less bad humor all the afternoon, and the defeat had not improved his temper. "I say you got in my way, and that is why I lost the race."

"And I say your statement isn't true," returned Jack sturdily.

"It is true! And I won't let you or anybody else say any different," said Bill Glutts. And then, in sudden passion, he stepped forward and gave Jack a shove which sent the oldest Rover boy flat on his back in a snowbank.

CHAPTER II

ABOUT THE ROVERS

The attack upon Jack Rover was so unexpected that he had no chance to save himself from going down into the snowbank. He went down so hard and the snow was so soft that for the moment he was almost covered and had to flounder around quite some to regain his feet.

"See here, Bill Glutts! what do you mean by attacking my cousin?" cried Randy, leaping forward and catching the bully by the arm.

"He had no right to talk to me the way he did," retorted Glutts. "Let go of me!" and he shook himself free.

"What Jack said was true," put in Fred quickly. "I was on the back of our bobsled and watched you nearly all the time. You came over on our side of the road at least three different times."

By this time half a dozen of the cadets were speaking at once, Carncross and several others upholding Bill Glutts. In the midst of the discussion Jack managed to regain his feet, and, leaping forward, he caught Bill Glutts firmly by both wrists.

Arthur M. Winfield

"Glutts, you listen to me," said he sternly, looking the bully in the eyes. "If I wasn't an officer at the Hall, I'd give you a sound thrashing for what you just did. As it is, I expect you to apologize or else take the consequences."

"Huh! I suppose you mean by that you'll play sissy and report me," said the bully.

"No, I won't report you, but I'll see to it that you get what is coming to you," answered Jack.

"Knowing he is an officer and can't fight you, you took a mean advantage of Jack," broke in Gif Garrison. "You ought to be thrashed for it, Glutts."

"I don't think Bill meant to shove him down into the snow," put in Codfish, somewhat timidly.

"He did mean to do it!" said Jack quickly. "And he'll either apologize for his actions or he'll take the consequences."

"Well, I'll take the consequences, whatever they are," retorted Bill Glutts, with a sickly grin. "I know that race wasn't a fair one. Come on, fellows, let's get back to the Hall, it's almost supper time," and with that he trudged away, he and his cronies pulling the *Yellow Streak* behind them.

"He sure is one sweet-tempered fellow," was Spouter's comment.

"Jack, why didn't you pitch into him, anyway?" questioned Andy anxiously.

"I didn't have to," returned Jack briefly. "Just the same, I won't forget the way he has acted. If it wasn't that I am captain of Company C, and am expected not to fight, I'd have given him the thrashing of his life."

To the many young folks who have read the former volumes in this series, the Rover boys will not need an introduction. But for the benefit of new readers a few words concerning my characters will be necessary.

In the first volume, entitled "The Rover Boys at School," I related how three brothers, Dick, Tom, and Sam Rover, were sent to Putnam Hall Military Academy, where they made a great number of friends, including a cadet named Lawrence Colby.

From Putnam Hall the boys went to Brill College, and, after leaving that institution of learning, joined their father in business in New York City, with offices on Wall Street. They organized The Rover Company, of which Dick was president, Tom, secretary and general manager, and Sam, treasurer.

During their cadet days at Putnam Hall the three Rovers had become acquainted with a number of charming girls, including Dora Stanhope and her cousins, Nellie and Grace Laning. When Dick went into business he made Dora Stanhope his life partner, and a short while after this Tom married Nellie Laning and Sam married Grace. The three brothers purchased a fine plot of ground on Riverside Drive overlooking the Hudson River, and there they built three connecting houses, Dick and his wife living in the middle house, with Tom on one side and Sam on the other.

About a year after their marriage Dick and his wife became the proud parents of a little son, who was named John after Mr. Laning. This son was followed by a daughter, named Martha, after her Great-aunt Martha, of Valley Brook Farm. Little Jack, as he was commonly called, was a manly lad with many of the qualities which made his father so successful in life.

It was about this time that Tom and Nellie Rover sprang a great surprise on all the others. This surprise was in the shape of a pair of very lively boy twins, one christened Anderson, after his grandfather, and the other Randolph, after his Great-uncle Randolph of Valley Brook Farm. Andy and Randy, as the twins were always called, were decidedly active lads, taking after their father, "who was never still a minute," to quote Grandpa Rover.

Shortly after the twins were born, Sam and Grace Rover came along with a beautiful girl, named Mary, after Mrs. Laning. Then, a year later, the girl was followed by a sturdy boy, who was called Fred, in honor of Sam Rover's old and well known school chum, Fred Garrison.

Residing so close together, the younger generation of Rovers were brought up very much like one big family. They usually spent their winters in New York City, and during the summers often went out to Valley Brook Farm, where their grandfather, Anderson Rover, still resided with Uncle Randolph and Aunt Martha.

When the boys and girls grew old enough they were at first sent to private schools in the Metropolis. But soon the lads, led by Andy and Randy, showed a propensity for "cutting loose" that their parents were compelled to hold a consultation.

"We'll have to send them to some strict boarding school—some military academy," said Dick Rover; and so it was decided.

Lawrence Colby, their old Putnam Hall chum, had since that

time become a colonel in the state militia and had then opened a military academy called Colby Hall. To this institution, Jack, Fred and the twins were sent, as related in detail in the first volume of my second series, entitled "The Rover Boys at Colby Hall."

This military school was located about half a mile from the town of Haven Point on Clearwater Lake, a beautiful sheet of water about two miles long. The school consisted of a large stone building facing the lake. It was a three-storied structure and contained the classrooms and the mess hall, and also dormitories and private rooms for the students. Besides the main building, there was a smaller structure occupied by Colonel Colby and his family and some of the professors, and also an up-to-date gymnasium and boathouses and bathing pavilions.

On arriving at the academy the younger Rovers found several of their friends awaiting them, one of these being Dick Powell, the son of Songbird Powell, a former schoolmate of their fathers. Dick was always called Spouter because of a fondness for long speeches. Another cadet was Gif Garrison, a son of Fred Garrison, after whom Fred Rover had been named. There was also Walter Baxter, a son of Dan Baxter, who, years previous, had been an enemy of the older Rovers, but who had since reformed and who was doing well.

As mentioned, Colby Hall was situated about half a mile from Haven Point. On the opposite side of the town was located Clearwater Hall, a boarding school for girls. During a panic in a moving picture theatre Jack and his cousins became acquainted with a number of these school girls, including Ruth Stevenson, May Powell, Alice Strobell and Annie Larkins. They soon found out that May was Spouter Powell's cousin, and the whole crowd of young people became friends. Later on Mary and Martha Rover became pupils at Clearwater Hall.

Ruth Stevenson had an old Uncle Barney, who in times past had had a bitter quarrel with Ruth's parents. The Rover boys, while out hunting one day, had occasion to save the old man's life. For this the old fellow was exceedingly grateful, and as a result he invited them to spend their winter holidays with him, which they did, as related in "The Rover Boys on Snowshoe Island."

On this island the lads met two of their former enemies, Nappy Martell and Slugger Brown, as well as Asa Lemm, a discharged teacher of Colby Hall. The boys exposed a plot against old Uncle Barney, and in the end caused the old fellow's enemies to leave in disgust.

"I guess we haven't seen the last of Nappy and Slugger," said Jack when he and his cousins had left Snowshoe Island.

And he was right. Nappy and Slugger turned up once more, as related in the volume previous to this, entitled "The Rover Boys Under Canvas." In that volume I told how the cadets went into their annual encampment, this being after a spirited election for officers in which Jack Rover had been elected captain of Company C and Fred had been elected first lieutenant of the same command.

Among the cadets who wished to become a captain was one named Gabe Werner, a great chum at that time of Bill Glutts. Having failed of election, Werner did all he could to make things uncomfortable for the Rovers, and in his actions he was seconded by Glutts. But in the end Werner and Glutts were discovered in some of their nefarious doings, and, becoming alarmed, Gabe Werner left the school camp early in the morning and did not return. Glutts was brought before

Captain Dale, the teacher in charge of the camp, and received a stern lecture and was deprived of many liberties he might otherwise have enjoyed. He laid his troubles at the door of the Rovers and vowed that sooner or later he would pay them back for the way he had been treated.

While the Rover boys were at Colby Hall the great war in Europe had opened and our country was now overrun with German spies and sympathizers. During their time at the encampment the boys made several surprising discoveries, and in the end helped the Secret Service officers to capture a hidden German submarine. They also rounded up the fathers of Nappy Martell and Slugger Brown. Mr. Brown and Mr. Martell were sent to prison, while Slugger and Nappy were marched off to a detention camp in the South, and that, for the time being, was the last the Rovers heard of them.

"Well, one thing is certain—we're well rid of Slugger and Nappy and their fathers," remarked Jack, as this news was brought to them.

"Yes, and I guess we're rid of Gabe Werner too," said Fred. "He seems to have dropped out completely." But in his remark concerning Werner the young lieutenant was mistaken. Gabe Werner was destined to turn up in their path unexpectedly and cause them not a little trouble.

When the call for volunteers came, Dick Rover and Sam had lost no time in enlisting. At first Tom Rover had been unable to get away. But now the business in New York City had been left in reliable hands, and all three fathers of the boys were in the trenches in Europe doing their bit for Uncle Sam. They had been in several small engagements, and so far had come through unwounded.

"But there is no telling if they will come through every

Arthur M. Winfield

time," was the way Fred expressed himself anxiously.

"Right you are," answered Jack. "Do you know, I dread to look at the lists of the killed and wounded in the newspapers for fear I'll see one of their names."

"Oh, if only this awful war was over!" put in Randy.

CHAPTER III

NEWS OF IMPORTANCE

"Battalion attention! Shoulder arms! Forward march!"

Boom! Boom! Boom, boom, boom! The drums beat, and away marched the three companies forming the Colby Hall battalion. They marched around the school building, as was the custom, and then marched into the place, put away their rifles, and entered the mess hall.

The roll call and brief drill and march took place less than half an hour after the encounter on the hill following the finish of the bobsled race. Captain Jack and Lieutenant Fred had lost no time in hurrying back to the school, and their chums had gone with them. Bill Glutts and his cronies had gone ahead, as already stated. And they did not show themselves until the call came to appear on the parade ground.

As captain and lieutenant, Jack and Fred were in rather a delicate position when it came to quarreling with the other cadets. In the past Colonel Colby had laid down the rule that there should be no fighting at the Hall, and this rule was particularly enforced when it came to officers. Now that the master of the military academy had joined the army and gone

Arthur M. Winfield

with the older Rovers to Europe, Captain Dale, who was in general command, was enforcing this rule with more strictness than ever before.

The afternoon spent coasting had given the Rovers and their chums good appetites, and they fell to with gusto over the ample supper provided for them. Unlike many boarding schools, the table at Colby Hall was always a bountiful one, and it is needless to say that the growing cadets always did full justice to everything that was set before them.

"What are you going to do about Bill Glutts, Jack?" questioned Fred, after the meal was over and the two were on their way to get several reference books from the school library.

"I don't know yet," was the young captain's answer. "He ought to have a thrashing, but you know how matters stand."

"Of course. And Jack, we can't think of that with the end of the term so near. You don't want to spoil your record, and neither do I."

"It's a confounded shame that Glutts didn't leave when Gabe Werner went," continued the oldest Rover boy. "They were two of a kind."

"Did you hear what Andy said—that he thought Glutts had a lot of German blood in him?"

"That might be. His face looks it, and the name sounds a little that way too."

"Andy and Randy both want to pitch into him," continued the young lieutenant.

"You warn them not to do it—at least, not until this term comes to an end," warned Jack. "They have been cutting up so much since last September that their averages are none too high as it is. They'd be mighty sorry if Captain Dale sent home a bad report about them. It would just about break Aunt Nellie's heart, I'm sure."

Having procured the reference books, the two made their way upstairs to the rooms occupied by them. The Rovers had a suite of four rooms, one of which was used as a sitting room and for studying. As they walked through the upper hallway they passed Nick Carncross and Bill Glutts. Glutts looked sourly at them but did not say a word, and they refused to notice the pair.

"I guess you've got their goat, Bill," remarked Carncross, as they passed on. "That race really belonged to you, and they know it."

"Of course it belonged to me," returned Glutts. "If they hadn't got in my way I'd have won with ease. There isn't a bobsled anywhere around that can beat the *Yellow Streak*."

"I'm glad you shoved him over in the snow, even if he is a captain," continued Carncross. "He's got too big an opinion of himself."

"He only got to be captain by a fluke, Nick. Gabe Werner should have had that office," continued Glutts.

"Is that why Werner left?" questioned Carncross curiously.

"Oh, no. He left because he got sick of the discipline around here. He said there was no chance for any fun," answered Glutts.

"Where is he now? Did his folks approve of his leaving school?"

"Oh, I guess they didn't care one way or the other. Old man Werner is pretty rich, and he didn't get his money by being educated either. So I guess he doesn't care much for education."

"Does he let Gabe have much spending money?"

"Quite a little—but, of course, not as much as Gabe would like to have. You know Gabe is a good deal of a sport." Bill Glutts' face lit up with satisfaction. "I expect we are going to have a bang-up time together during the holidays."

"Then you expect to see him?"

"Yes; we're planning a trip together."

"Gee! I'll envy you," returned Carncross.

Andy and Randy had not yet come upstairs. Neither could resist the temptation to have a little fun, and after supper they had gone outside and begun to snowball Shout Plunger, the school janitor, and Bob Nixon, the chauffeur.

"It's all in fun, you know," explained Andy, as he let fly a snowball at the old janitor, who was always called Shout because he was so deaf.

"Hi there! you stop that!" roared Shout. And then, when they continued to snowball him, he came after them with a wooden snow-shovel.

"Look out! Here comes the enemy!" cried Randy gayly, and let fly a snowball which struck the upraised snow-shovel and sent a shower of loose snow into the janitor's face.

"You young rascals!" roared Plunger, and then lost his footing on some ice. In endeavoring to keep his balance he sent the snow-shovel whirling through the air. It landed at Andy's feet, catching that fun-loving youth in the shins and sending him flat on his face.

"Hurrah! One down!" came from Bob Nixon good-naturedly, and then the chauffeur picked up a large chunk of snow and threw it high in the air, to land directly on Randy's shoulder.

"Great pyramids of Egypt!" gasped Randy. "Is that a snowslide?" For some of the snow had filled his ear and gone down his neck.

"Oh, we didn't begin this, you know," cried the chauffeur gleefully. "Come on, Shout; let's show 'em what the older generation can do." And then he picked up another chunk of snow and hurled it at Andy, nearly burying that youth while he was endeavoring to regain his feet.

"Hi! Hi you!" spluttered Andy. "We went in for snowballing. We didn't go in for avalanches."

"When you start something, always be sure you can finish it," admonished Bob Nixon. And then he picked up a third chunk of snow; but before he could make use of it the Rover twins had dived out of sight around a corner of the school building.

"I guess that's the time we got the worst of it," remarked Andy ruefully.

"And maybe we deserved it," was Randy's ready response. "Come on and snowball some of the other cadets."

A number were willing, and an impromptu snowballing battle took place which lasted the best part of a quarter of an hour. Then one of the teachers came out and ordered the youths upstairs, for this was the study hour.

On Sundays such of the cadets as desired to do so were permitted to attend one or another of the churches in Haven Point. All of the Rovers went to church, and there met, not only Mary and Martha, but also Ruth Stevenson, May Powell, and some of the other girls.

"Well, Jack, I suppose this snowy weather puts you in mind of the time you went to my Uncle Barney's place on Snowshoe Island," remarked Ruth Stevenson, with a bright smile at the young captain, who, of course, was dressed in his best uniform.

"That's what it does, Ruth," he answered. "And, my, what a good time we did have! How is your uncle getting along?"

"Very well indeed. He is a changed man since he stopped quarreling with my folks and since it has been proved that Snowshoe Island is really and truly his property."

"I'm glad we were able to help the old man."

"Have you decided on what you intend to do during the coming holidays?" continued the girl from Clearwater Hall.

"Not exactly, Ruth. More than likely we'll go home with the girls and spend some time with our mothers. They probably feel pretty lonely now that our dads have gone to Europe."

"Yes, I can imagine how that must be."

"You girls ought to come down with Mary and Martha."

"We're talking of doing that," put in May Powell. "You see, we wanted them to come up to my house first, and then Ruth wanted them. But as their mothers are now all alone in New York they thought it best that we should spend the time down there. We could have something of a house party, and that would help cheer the older folks up."

"A good idea!" came from Fred. "Do it by all means!"

"Yes, you girls can have a fine time in New York during the winter holidays," added Randy.

"I suppose you boys will want to go off hunting," said May, pouting a little. "I wish I was a boy and could do that!"

"Gee! I wish we could go off hunting, like we did that time at Snowshoe Island," cried Randy wistfully. "Such an outing would suit me right down to the ground."

"Gif Garrison said something a few days ago about going off on a hunt," remarked Fred. "He says his father some years ago bought a place known as Cedar Lodge. He didn't tell me very much about it. In fact, he acted quite mysteriously."

"I suppose he didn't want to hurt your feelings, Fred," returned Jack. "More than likely he knew you would feel bad to have him going off for a good time up in the woods and have you and the rest of us staying at home."

Two days passed, and the young cadets were so busy getting ready for the examinations previous to the midwinter holidays that they had no time to pay attention to anything else. They heard that Bill Glutts was openly boasting that the *Yellow Streak* could beat any bobsled in that vicinity and that the *Blue Moon* had won the contest by a foul. But to this just then they paid no attention.

"I'll get at Bill later—just wait!" was the way Jack expressed himself, and the others knew that the young captain would keep his word.

On Wednesday the boys received letters from home stating that word had come in that their fathers were still in the trenches in France. No serious fighting had so far taken place in their sector, and none of them had been wounded and all were in the best of health.

"That's the best news yet," said Fred, with satisfaction, and the others agreed with him.

Gif Garrison had also received a letter, and this he read with tremendous satisfaction. His face was aglow as he called the Rover boys to him.

"I've got an important announcement to make to you fellows," he said. "Let us go up to your rooms and talk it over."

"What is the announcement?" questioned Andy eagerly.

"I'll tell you when we are alone," answered Gif.

CHAPTER IV

SOMETHING ABOUT CEDAR LODGE

"Oh, go ahead, Gif, and get it off your chest!"

"Don't keep us waiting."

"Has some one died and left you a fortune?"

Such were some of the remarks made after Gif Garrison had said that he had an important announcement to make to the four Rover boys.

"Not another word until we get to your rooms," said Gif. "And, Andy, won't you please run off and get Spouter Powell? I just saw him heading for the gymnasium."

"All right, Gif. But don't you dare to let the others in on the secret until I get back," returned the fun-loving Rover boy, and away he sped on his errand.

A few minutes later all of the lads mentioned were assembled in the Rover boys' sitting room, some on chairs, one on a table, and two on a couch. Andy playfully started to throw a pillow at Fred, but Gif at once put up his hand in protest.

Arthur M. Winfield

"Any horseplay, and I'll call it all off," he warned.

"I'll be good, Gif!" cried Andy reluctantly, and got rid of the pillow by using it for a back rest.

"This letter is from my Uncle Louis, who is a partner with my father in the ownership of a large tract of land not far from the seacoast," began Gif. "There is a small but comfortable bungalow on it, known as Cedar Lodge. Nobody was going to use the Lodge this winter, and I suggested to my folks and Uncle Louis that they allow us fellows to occupy it during the holidays."

"And what did they say?" questioned Randy eagerly.

"They said I could go there if I wanted to, and I could take you Rover boys and Spouter with me, provided you could get consent to go."

"Isn't that dandy!"

"Of course we'll go, Gif. Horses couldn't hold us back!"

"How is the hunting there? Can we get a deer or a moose?"

"How do you get there?"

These were a few questions hurled at Gif after he had made his important announcement. He placed his hands over his ears in despair.

"One question at a time, please!" he begged. "What do you think I am, anyhow—an encyclopaedia? To get there you go from here to Portview, and then along the coast to a place called Timminsport. From Timminsport you have either to take a sleigh or else hike to the camp, which is about five or six miles away. There is an old fellow, named Jed Wallop, who lives near the property in a little shack some distance from the bungalow. If we want him to, he will get a sled and drive us to the place, and he will also assist us in getting settled, and in getting what stores we may need—that is, provided you fellows can really go."

"You can count of me," declared Spouter promptly. "My folks said I could do as I pleased during the holidays, provided I kept out of mischief. And what mischief could a fellow get into in the midst of those grand primeval forests where perhaps the woodsman has never dared to lay his axe to the heart of the sturdy oak, and where the timid deer, in fancied freedom, ambles through the darkening glades, and—"

"Turn off the spigot, Spouter, or you'll have us flooded!" burst out Randy.

"Save your orations for the day before election," came from Fred.

"You can give us the rest of it, Spouter, when we are in camp some night and have nothing to read and don't know what to do," suggested Jack.

"That's it—always cutting my rhetorical effusions short," remarked Spouter reproachfully. "Some day, when you are aching to have me make a speech, you'll find me dumb."

"Tell us more about this camp, Gif," cried Fred.

Thereupon Gif Garrison related all he knew concerning the camp, which was located on a small stream of water that in the summer time ran down to a bay emptying into the Atlantic Ocean. There was a good deal of timber on the tract, and, so far as Gif knew, there was quite some small game.

"I don't know about deer," he continued. "More than likely the big animals have gone further north. But one might get a chance at a wolf or a fox, and maybe some brook mink. We'll be sure to get plenty of rabbits and squirrels and ducks, and most likely some partridges and maybe wild turkeys. But, first of all, you Rovers have got to make sure that you can go."

"Oh, we'll arrange that somehow, Gif," said Jack. "Of course, we'll want to go home first and see our folks and cheer them up a bit. They are pretty lonely now that our dads are over in France."

"Oh, I'm going home myself first. But we can have at least three weeks up there, because the school is going to be closed more than a month before and after Christmas."

Gif's announcement was such a pleasing one that the Rovers found it hard work after that to settle down to their studies. Letters were at once written to their mothers, and presently word came back that they might go to the camp immediately after Christmas if they wanted to do so. Then Jack telephoned to his sister at Clearwater Hall and got word back that Ruth and May would go down to New York with Mary and Martha and remain there until it was time to return to the girls' school.

"It's too bad we can't be at home while the girls are there," remarked Jack to his cousins. He sighed deeply.

"You mean it's too bad you can't be there while Ruth is there," put in Andy slyly.

"That's the time you struck the nail on the head!" cried Randy.

"Humph! you needn't rap me about it," returned the young captain briefly. "I guess you'd like to see the girls yourselves."

Now that they knew what they were going to do during the midwinter holidays, the Rover boys and their chums were eager to have the school session come to an end. But they did not neglect their studies, nor did Jack and Fred neglect their duties as officers.

Jack had an essay to write on "The Real Training of a Soldier," and he spent a great deal of time over this.

"Not but what there is a good deal about it that I don't know," said Jack to his cousins. "I guess dad could write a better essay than I can turn out. He's seen some of the real side of a soldier's life."

"What wonderful things our dads will have to tell when they get back," said Fred. "That is, if they ever do get back," he added anxiously.

"Oh, they've got to come back, Fred! They've simply got to!" returned Jack. But his face, too, showed his worry. The Rover boys did not care to admit it to each other, yet each day every one of them worried over their parents. It was dreadful to think that one's father, or one's beloved uncle, might be killed by the Germans, or even badly wounded.

On the Saturday following the bobsled contest the boys assembled once more on the long Hill, and this time they were accompanied by many of the girls from Clearwater Hall. Jack and his cousins gave Ruth and the others many rides down the hill, much to their mutual delight.

"Here comes Bill Glutts with his *Yellow Streak*," cried

Arthur M. Winfield

Fred presently.

"Here's a chance to have another race with him, Jack," said Fatty Hendry. "He says you won the other race by a foul."

"That's the talk, Jack!" cried Dan Soppinger. "Show him and the whole crowd that you beat him fairly."

At first Jack did not care to pit himself again against Glutts. But there was so much talk that at length he consented, but insisted upon it that the whole course of the slide must be policed by the cadets.

"All right, we'll do that," said Major Ralph Mason, and then ordered all the cadets he could collect to station themselves on each side of the slide from the top to where it ran out on the lake.

"Oh, Jack, I hope you do win again!" said Ruth anxiously.

"I intend to do my best," he answered.

"You have got to win, Jack Rover!" cried his sister Martha. "If you don't beat that great big clumsy Glutts, I'll never speak to you again."

With so many cadets stationed along the course, Bill Glutts felt that his chances of winning the race were diminishing. He had thought that he could crowd Jack as he had done before, but now Walt Baxter laid down the law in such a manner that it could not be misunderstood.

"I will toss up a coin," said Walt, "and if you guess right, Glutts, you can take your choice of sides, and whichever side you or Jack Rover select, that side you must stick to from start to finish."

The coin was tossed up, and Bill Glutts called out "tails" and won. Then he said he would take the right side of the slide, that which Jack Rover and his chums had previously used.

"All right, then, Glutts," announced Walt. "Now then, remember that you have got to keep to the right all the way down; and you, Jack Rover, must keep to the left. If either of you crosses the middle of the course, that one will be disqualified and the race will be given to the other."

"All right, Walt, I will stick to the left from start to finish; just watch me and see," declared Jack.

"And I'll stick to the right," announced Bill Glutts. But his face showed anything but a happy expression as he spoke.

Jack had the same crowd on board that he had before, but Glutts made several changes. He retained Nick Carncross and Codfish, but for the other three cadets substituted youths who were slightly built, and consequently rather light in weight.

"He's saving all the pounds he can," whispered Randy.

"Jack, do you think the right side of the course is better than the left?" questioned Gif.

"I don't know. One looks about as good as the other to me," was the young captain's reply.

Professor Frank Grawson had come up and was quite interested in the proposed contest.

"I used to do a lot of bobsledding myself," said the professor, who was well liked by nearly all the cadets. "I used to have a home-made sled which was my pride for several seasons.

Now, to make this more interesting, I'll put up a prize for the winner."

"Fine, Professor! Fine!" was the cry.

"What's the prize?"

The teacher thought for a moment.

"Well, every boy likes a good pocket knife," he said presently. "Now, to the one who wins this race I'll give a first-class, four-bladed, buck-handled knife. I saw some very good ones down in the hardware store at the Point, and I'll get one Monday."

"That's splendid, Professor!" cried Jack. "I'll do my best to win that knife."

"You'll see that knife coming to me!" exclaimed Bill Glutts, glaring at the young captain.

Walt Baxter now called for the contestants to get ready. In a minute more the two bobsleds stood side by side, each with its load of passengers, and with Fred ready to push one to the front and Nick Carncross ready to shove the other.

"All ready!" shouted Walt. "One—two—three! Go!"

And away both bobsleds dashed, and the great race was on.

CHAPTER V

THE DEFEAT OF THE BULLY

"Go ahead, Jack! You've got to win!"

"Don't let 'em beat you, Bill. Put it all over those Rovers."

"Oh, Jack, don't let them get the best of you!" cried Ruth.

"You've got to win!" screamed Martha.

"Here is where Glutts shows 'em what the *Yellow Streak* can do!"

So the cries ran on as the two bobsleds slowly gathered momentum and started down the long slope leading to Clearwater Lake.

At the beginning Glutts had a little the better of it, because the right side of the slide seemed to be more slippery than the other. He was the first to gain the top of the nearest rise and he shot over this while Jack's bobsled was still climbing the slope.

"Hurrah! Bill Glutts is ahead!"

Arthur M. Winfield

"He said the *Yellow Streak* could beat any thing in this vicinity."

"Oh, do you really think Glutts will win?" questioned Ruth anxiously, as she turned to Dan Soppinger.

"Well, I should hope not!" answered Dan.

"If he does win there will be no holding him down," put in Ned Lowe, another chum of the Rovers. "He'll crow to beat the band all winter."

Forward went the two bobsleds, each steersman doing his best to guide his sled where running might be the easiest.

Just as Jack topped the first rise and started to speed down on the other side, he saw Bill Glutts start to resume his old tactics. The bully was running close to the center of the course, and now he overlapped the other side by at least six inches.

"Hi, there, Glutts! Get over on your side!" yelled one of the cadets who was helping to police the course.

"That's right, Bill. Get over, or you'll be disqualified," added another.

"Keep to the right! Keep to the right!" was the cry from several others. And then, knowing that the eyes of all the cadets in that vicinity were upon him, the bully slowly steered over to his side of the course. And he was not any too quick, for otherwise there might have been a serious disaster. Down the slope of the first hill rushed the *Blue Moon*. Jack was on his side, but had not more than six inches to spare. Had Glutts kept on as he was running the *Blue Moon* would have sideswiped the *Yellow Streak*, and there would undoubtedly have been a serious accident.

"Here comes the *Blue Moon*!"

"Say, but they are gathering some speed!"

"Hurrah, the Rovers are ahead!"

"Go on, Glutts! Go on! Don't let 'em beat you!"

It was true that the *Blue Moon* was now ahead and was slowly but surely increasing the distance between the Rovers and those aboard the *Yellow Streak*.

"Push her ahead, Bill! Push her ahead!" yelled Nick Carncross desperately.

"We've got to win!" cried Codfish.

"I'm doing the best I can," muttered Bill Glutts between his set teeth, and his eyes glowed with hatred as he saw the *Blue Moon* vanishing over the second rise of the course.

After that, as Fatty Hendry remarked, "it was all over but the shouting." Down toward the highway skirting the lake shot the *Blue Moon*. Then it ran swiftly along the final lap of the course and came out on Clearwater Lake, shooting several hundred feet beyond the finishing mark. The line was crossed while the *Yellow Streak* was still on the roadway beyond the lake shore.

"Hurrah! The *Blue Moon* wins!"

"My, but that was some run, believe me!"

"What will Bill Glutts have to say now?"

"He can't say this wasn't a fair race."

The run for the *Blue Moon* had certainly been a swift one, and while Jack was congratulated on his victory, he was also praised for the way in which he had handled his speedy bobsled.

"We certainly came down fast," remarked Randy. "I thought my ears were going to blow right off my head," and this remark caused a general laugh.

Glutts had finished the race twelve seconds behind his opponent and was in anything but a happy frame of mind.

"There were a number of sticks and stones on my side of the slide, and they held us back," he protested lamely. "I guess some of the fellows who didn't want to see the *Yellow Streak* win put 'em there."

"I can't believe that, Glutts," answered Major Mason flatly. "I looked over the course, and it was just as clear on one side as it was on the other."

"Don't be a sorehead, Bill, just because you lost," put in Fatty Hendry. "Be a good sport and shake hands with Jack over your defeat."

"I'll do as I please," roared the bully. "I don't need any advice from you. You fellows are all against me." And with this remark he turned his back on the crowd, and soon he and his cronies were making their way up along the lake shore, dragging the *Yellow Streak* behind them.

"It was a well won race, Captain Rover," said Professor Grawson. "You can be proud of being the possessor of such a speedy bobsled. On Monday I shall take great pleasure in getting that knife for you."

"Thank you, Professor. And I'll take great pleasure in accepting the knife," said Jack, with a grin.

"Well, that's the time you squared up with Bill Glutts," remarked Spouter, after the fun on Long Hill had come to an end and the boys had said good-bye to the girls and were on the return to Colby Hall. "You certainly paid him back for shoving you into that snowbank."

"I don't know whether I did or not," answered the young captain. "Evidently Glutts doesn't know when he's had enough. I suppose he'll be more bitter now than ever against me."

"Oh, I wouldn't worry about Glutts," put in Gif. "He's nothing but a great big overgrown butcher boy." He said this because it was a well-known fact that Bill Glutts was the only son of a wholesale butcher who had made a small fortune in manufacturing and selling frankfurters.

"I don't see how a fellow like Nick Carncross can take up with him," remarked Fatty Hendry.

"I know why he does that," came from Ned Lowe. "Bill has had plenty of money to spend lately—an uncle or somebody sent him quite a wad—and Nick's pocketbook, I imagine, is rather thin."

"Say, Ned, come around to our rooms to-night and give us some music just to celebrate this glorious event!" cried Fred, for Ned Lowe was quite a performer on the mandolin and usually had some very funny songs to sing.

"All right, I'll be glad to come," answered the mandolin

player. "Any eats?"

"Oh, maybe we can scrape up something," answered Randy. The idea of a little spread on the quiet appealed to him.

The idea of a little spread appealed to the others, too, and as a consequence it was arranged between the Rovers and their chums that two of them should go to Haven Point for some things for the spread. This task was delegated to Andy and Fred, and they hurried off early in the evening, returning with several packages containing sandwiches, cake, candy, nuts and a large hand of bananas. In the meantime, the other Rover boys and Ned Lowe had gathered in Gif Garrison's room, and there enjoyed themselves singing and listening to Ned's playing of the mandolin.

As soon as the monitors had gone their rounds to see that everything was quiet for the night, Spouter, Gif, Fatty, Ned, Dan, Walt and several others found their way to the Rover boys' suite.

"Now, don't make too much noise," admonished Fred, who let them in. "Remember Bill Glutts and his gang will be only too glad to find out what is going on and report us."

"And we don't want to get any black marks when it's so near the end of the term," added Jack.

"Right-o," came from Andy.

The new arrivals proceeded to make themselves at home, and then the Rovers passed around the good things which had been obtained.

"Say, this is all right," declared Walt, munching a tongue sandwich.

"Couldn't be beat," came from Gif, who had his mouth full of layer cake.

"Here, Fatty, have some nuts!" cried Andy gayly, and let several almonds slide down the fat youth's collar.

"Hi, there! Let up!" cried Fatty. "I don't eat nuts that way," and he made a pass at Andy with a pillow.

"No horseplay, now! Cut it out, Andy," warned Jack.

After that the cadets conversed in low tones and at the same time enjoyed the many good things to eat.

"What are you going to do with those banana skins, Andy?" questioned his twin, as he saw the youth place several of the skins in a bit of newspaper.

"Oh, I've got a plan to use them," was the answer.

"Well, if there is any fun on foot, let me in on it," went on Randy promptly.

"I was thinking we might send some of these good things over to Bill Glutts, Codfish and Nick Carncross," went on the fun-loving Rover. "It might make 'em feel better over their defeat."

"What! Give up some of these good eats to them?" demanded Fred.

"Well, I don't know whether they would be very good eats or not," answered Andy, closing one eye suggestively. "Do you see what I've got in this little package?" he went on, bringing a small paper bag from his pocket. "Smell it."

Arthur M. Winfield

Fred did so, but with caution. Then he gave a sudden sneeze.

"Cayenne pepper!"

"Right you are, Freddie boy! How did you guess it?" and Andy grinned broadly.

"Say, that's the talk!" burst out Randy. "Let's send them over a few sandwiches and a couple of slices of cake, all well doctored with cayenne pepper."

"They'll be suspicious, especially if you take them over," remarked Jack. "We ought to get some outsider to do the job."

"I'll do it if you want me too," responded Walt Baxter promptly. "I don't love those chaps any more than you do. You just fix up some sandwiches and the cake, and I'll go around and explain that Dan and Ned and Fatty, and some of the rest of us, are giving the Rovers a little spread in honor of the victory and that we don't think it any more than right that they should have some of the good things."

So it was decided, and a little while later the cover of a pasteboard box was fixed up as a tray, containing several tempting looking sandwiches, some slices of layer cake, and two bananas. Then Walt Baxter marched off with the things in the direction of the room occupied by Bill Glutts.

"Come on and listen to what happens," said Andy, and presently, having slipped off their shoes, he and the others followed Walt down the corridor, but kept well in the background.

When Baxter arrived at Bill Glutts' room he heard low voices, and was much pleased to learn that Glutts was talking to Nick Carncross. When he knocked lightly on the door there was an uneasy stir within.

"Maybe it's one of the monitors come back," whispered Carncross uneasily.

"Who is there?" questioned Glutts sharply.

"It's I—Walt Baxter," was the answer. "Open the door, Glutts. I've got something good for you fellows."

The door was opened cautiously, and Walt explained his errand, at the same time holding out the improvised tray.

"I don't know that we want anything," said Glutts rather sourly.

"Oh, well, we might as well take it," put in Carncross hastily. He was a growing cadet, and always hungry.

"We'd like to have Codfish have some of this, too," said Walt. "Will you see that he gets some?"

"Sure!" answered Carncross readily. "He's right across the hall. I'll call him."

In a few minutes more Codfish came from his room clad in his pajamas and slippers. He sneaked over into the room occupied by Glutts and Carncross, and then the three began dividing the things Walt had brought for them.

"I'll have to go now," said Walt hastily. "Remember, this is with regards from our whole crowd," he added significantly.

"Thanks," muttered Carncross briefly, while Glutts and Codfish said nothing.

Then the bully closed the door and he and his cronies prepared to enjoy the things which had been brought to them.

CHAPTER VI

AT THE MOVING PICTURE THEATRE

"There'll be something doing in a minute or two," murmured Randy, as he and the others came to a halt before Bill Glutts' door.

"You fellows be careful and don't step on any of these," whispered Andy, as he bent down and laid the banana skins he had saved on the floor. "Splendid doormat for them when they come out," he added, grinning.

Fortunately, those within the room were so busy dividing the sandwiches and cake that they paid no attention to what was going on outside.

"Rather nice of them to remember us," remarked Codfish. "Thank you, I don't think I care for any sandwiches, but I'll take that piece of cake instead."

"Me for a sandwich, Bill," murmured Carncross. "I'm quite hungry."

Then the three began to munch away on the sandwiches and the cake at a lively rate.

All had their mouths full when suddenly Codfish began to splutter.

"Hello! what's the matter?" cried Glutts. "Trying to swallow too much at once?"

"You don't want to make a pig of yourself, Codfish," admonished Carncross.

"Oh! Oh!" cried the sneak of the school. "Oh!"

"What's wrong?"

"Oh, I'm burning up! Oh, they must have poisoned me!"

"Gee! do you suppose they put something in that cake?" cried Carncross, in sudden alarm.

"Oh, my mouth is on fire!" groaned Codfish.

To this neither Glutts nor Carncross made any answer. Each was beginning to feel a sudden strange sensation on his tongue and in his throat. Both began to feel as if their mouths were burning up.

"It's something they've put in the eats!" exclaimed Glutts. "They're trying to poison us, or something!"

"It's pepper! That's what it is—cayenne pepper!" came from Codfish. "Oh, give me a drink of water, or something! This is dreadful!"

The sneak made a dash across the room to where a water pitcher stood on a stand with a glass beside it. But the pitcher proved to be empty.

"My gracious, this is terrible!" spluttered Carncross, and began to cough.

In the meantime Glutts smelled of the food that remained on the improvised tray, and suddenly gave a loud sneeze, followed by several others.

"Hurrah! they are enjoying it all right enough," remarked Jack, in a low tone.

"I've got to have a drink!" yelled Carncross recklessly. "Gee! I'm burning up clean from my mouth to my stomach!"

"You're no worse off than I am," spluttered Glutts. "Oh, just wait until I get hold of that Walt Baxter!"

"It was the whole bunch that did it. I'll bet the trick was gotten up by those Rovers!"

The door was flung open, and all of the occupants of the room dashed out into the hallway, bent upon getting to the nearest bathroom or water cooler for a drink. Not one of them noticed the slippery banana skins spread out on the floor, and on the instant Bill Glutts went sliding along and came down flat on his back. Carncross did likewise, Codfish tripping over him and pitching headlong.

"Say! what's this?" exploded Glutts. "Oh, my back! I guess I've broken my shoulder."

"They must have soaked the floor," came from Carncross. "No! It's banana skins," he added, in deep disgust. "Say, Codfish, take your feet off my stomach, will you?"

"I—I couldn't help falling over you, you went down so suddenly," apologized the sneak. "Oh dear! let me get a drink

Arthur M. Winfield

of water—I'm all on fire inside."

The Rovers and their chums had retreated to a distance, and this was wise, for, had Glutts and Carncross been able to get hold of them, there would certainly have been a fight. But as it was, the bully and his cronies passed down a back corridor to the nearest bathroom, where they proceeded to wash out their mouths and get a long drink.

"Now we'd better get back to our rooms and get into bed as soon as possible," said Jack. "They may report us, and some of the professors may come around to investigate."

"Let them come! We'll all be asleep like so many innocent lambs," remarked Randy.

"They'll find that I've been asleep for the last two hours," added Walt Baxter, and at this the others had to smile.

The crowd separated, and the four Rovers returned to their rooms, where they lost no time in getting rid of all the evidences of the feast. Then they undressed, turned out the lights, and crept into their beds.

"I don't believe they'll dare to report this," whispered Andy to his twin. And in this surmise the fun-loving Rover was correct. Glutts and his cronies did a good deal of grumbling, but there the matter, for the time being, ended.

"But I'll get square some day! You just wait and see!" Glutts told the others.

The school term was now drawing to an end, and it was definitely announced that, owing to the war conditions, Colby Hall would remain closed for a period of six weeks for the winter holidays. This would give the Rovers and their chums a full month's vacation after New Year's.

"And what a good time we will have up at Cedar Lodge!" cried Fred.

"It certainly was grand of Gif to ask us to go up there with him and Spouter," added Jack.

The Rovers and their chums, and especially Walt Baxter, kept a close eye on Bill Glutts and his cronies. But beyond scowling at them whenever they passed, the bully did nothing regarding the peppered food which had been presented.

"He's laying low for something, I suppose," said Walt. "However, I'm not going to worry."

One day he received a "soaker" of a snowball in his left ear while hurrying to the gymnasium. He did not know who threw the missile, but was satisfied in his mind that it came from either Glutts or Carncross.

The examinations for the term were held, and much to the Rover boys' satisfaction all acquitted themselves creditably. Spouter and Gif did very well too, and were equally elated.

"Let us go down to town this evening and celebrate," suggested Jack that afternoon. "I think Captain Dale will let us go, and I understand they are giving a very good war picture at Mr. Falstein's moving picture theater."

"That will suit me," answered Fred.

The matter was talked over by a number of the cadets, and they went to see Captain Dale about it; and as a result nine of them set out for Haven Point, where was located the moving

Arthur M. Winfield

picture theater at which Jack and his cousins first met the girls from Clearwater Hall.

"This looks like a pretty good picture," remarked Gif, as he pointed to one advertised on the billboards. "A real war play with some of the scenes taken at the front."

"Either at the front or on the Hackensack Meadows," remarked Randy dryly. "They tell me that more than three-fourths of those so-called war pictures are faked up."

"Well, you wouldn't expect the moving picture actors to go right out in the middle of a battlefield and perform, would you?" queried Jack.

"Here's a good comic, too!" put in Fatty Hendry. "That suits me all right. I like a good laugh."

"Fatty, you ought to go in the movies," remarked Fred. "You would make a hit as the Living Skeleton."

"He would unless his face broke the camera," added Ned Lowe.

"I understand some of those fat fellows in the movies get a couple of hundred dollars a week for acting," said Fatty. "I wouldn't mind doing some of those stunts myself at that price."

The cadets purchased their tickets and were soon inside the showhouse. An educational film was being thrown on the screen, and they were much interested in seeing the details of tanning leather and making leather belts, handbags, and shoes.

"Gee! how easy it is to learn about these things in a moving picture," remarked Gif.

"What a pity it is they can't teach a fellow algebra and geometry in the same way," sighed Randy.

The educational film was followed by the war play, and whether this was given with faked-up backgrounds or not, it proved to be a very interesting production, especially to the Rover boys. There were pictures of life in the soldiers' camps and on the transports bound for Europe, and then scenes of life in the French trenches, culminating in a terrific bombardment by big cannons, and then a thrilling charge over No-Man's Land.

"Gee, isn't that immense!" murmured Fred. "Think of dad being in such a charge as that!"

"It brings the war pretty close, doesn't it, Fred?" asked Jack.

The scenes of the mighty conflict not alone thrilled the Rover boys but also sobered them, especially when there came a picture of the dead and the dying, with the ambulances rushing hither and thither to take the wounded to the field hospitals.

Poor Fred felt the tears coming into his eyes, and was glad that the moving picture house was rather dark, so that he might use his handkerchief without being noticed.

The war picture was followed immediately by one depicting the trials and tribulations of a fat man who obtained a position as a bell-boy in a country hotel. He did some wonderful stunts, and managed to break up a great deal of crockeryware and innumerable pies, and this set all the cadets, as well as the majority of the audience, to roaring with laughter.

"I guess those fellows earn their money," remarked Spouter to Fatty. "Just think of being slammed around in front of the camera like that!"

"Yes. And think of having three or four pies plastered all over your face," returned the stout youth. "I guess, after all, I'd rather go into ordinary business."

"I imagine some of those so-called stunts are only trick pictures—I mean those things like climbing up the side of a house and holding on to the top of a church steeple," remarked Jack. "Just the same, those moving picture actors have to risk their lives more than once, especially when they take wild rides on horse-back or in automobiles, or get in railroad smash-ups."

Immediately following the comic picture, all the lights in the theater were turned on and a gentleman stepped on the stage to address the audience.

"I wonder what he's going to talk about," whispered Randy.

"Liberty Loan, or something like that, I suppose," answered his twin.

He was right. There was a new drive on to raise money for the Government to be used for war purposes, and this gentleman, as a member of the local committee, had come forth to urge every man and woman in the audience to invest in Liberty Bonds.

"That is what my father was doing in and around New York before he went to war," explained Andy to Walt Baxter. "He made quite a success of it, too. He was on a whole lot of committees."

"And he did a lot of work for the Red Cross, too," added Randy.

While the lights were turned on the cadets had a chance to look around the showhouse. They thought that possibly some of the girls from Clearwater Hall might be present, but they were disappointed.

The talk about Liberty Bonds had come to an end, and several men and women were passing through the audience trying to get subscribers for the bonds when half a dozen newcomers entered the moving picture theater. One of the number was in cadet uniform, and as he came down the aisle and took a seat on the other side of the showhouse, Jack caught Fred by the arm.

"Look who's here, will you?" he whispered excitedly.

"Why, it's Bill Glutts!" returned Fred.

"Exactly! And do you see who is with him?"

"No. I can't make out. Who is it?"

"Gabe Werner!"

"Gabe Werner! Are you sure, Jack?"

"Positive! I saw him full in the face just before he sat down."

Soon the lights in the showhouse went out once more, and the moving picture performance continued.

Arthur M. Winfield

CHAPTER VII

THE END OF THE TERM

"What can Gabe Werner be doing around here?" questioned Randy, who had heard the conversation between his two cousins.

"I'm sure I don't know," answered Jack. "He doesn't live anywhere in this vicinity, and I thought after he left the school he went home."

"Evidently Glutts must have known about his being here, otherwise they wouldn't be together," said Andy.

Jack stood up so that he might get a better view of the other side of the showhouse. He noticed several vacant seats directly behind those occupied by Glutts and Werner.

"I'm going to slip over there just as soon as the lights are turned down," he said to Fred. "If they are hatching out any mischief perhaps we'll hear something worth listening to."

"I'll go with you," was the ready reply.

The pair explained to the others what they were about to do, and then slipped out of their seats and made their way to the back of the moving picture theater. Then, when the lights were being turned out, they moved forward and slipped into two seats directly behind Glutts and Werner without being noticed by the two bullies.

The educational film was now being shown again, and this caused Glutts to give a snort of disgust.

"I don't care for that sort of stuff," said the wholesale butcher's son. "I wish they would put on the war play. Tell me some more about this scheme you've got for spending the winter holidays."

"Oh, it's a dandy scheme, all right, Bill," responded Werner. And then he began a description of a winter's camp and told how he had permission to go there and how he wanted Glutts to go with him.

While Gabe Werner was speaking some people sitting next to him had arisen and were trying to get out. Gabe and Bill arose, and as they did so the former turned around and caught sight of the two Rovers.

"Say! what do you know about this?" he cried in astonishment.

"Jack Rover and Fred Rover!" murmured Glutts, and his face likewise betrayed astonishment.

"Did you fellows follow us into the theater?" demanded Werner.

"We certainly did not," returned Fred quickly. "We were in the theater long before you came in."

"Huh!" Werner was stumped for a moment. "I didn't notice

Arthur M. Winfield

them here, did you?" he questioned his crony.

"If I had I should have taken a seat elsewhere," was Glutts' ready reply. He glared at the Rovers. "I suppose you have been listening to everything we said."

"If you don't want to be heard you had better not talk in a place like this," replied Jack.

"I don't care what they did hear," grumbled Werner. "I'm not ashamed of what I am doing or intend to do."

"If I were you, Glutts, I'd cut Werner," advised Fred. "Captain Dale won't give you any credit for sticking to him after what happened at the encampment."

"I suppose you are going to tell Captain Dale you saw me with him," retorted Glutts.

"I shan't say a word unless I am questioned."

"I haven't forgotten what happened at the encampment," said Gabe Werner, turning to Jack. "Some day I'm going to square accounts with you."

"When that time comes I think I'll be able to defend myself, Werner," answered the young captain coldly.

By this time a number of people in the audience were turning around, evidently annoyed by the conversation. One heavy-set man turned back and tapped Werner on the shoulder.

"Say, if you fellows want to hold a talk-fest, go outside and do it," he growled. "We want to look at the pictures."

"Come ahead, Jack," whispered Fred. "It won't do us any

good to stay here, now that Glutts and Werner have discovered our presence."

"Right you are," was the answer. And a moment later the two Rovers slipped out of their seats and made their way to the rear of the showhouse. Here they were joined by the others of their crowd; and all went outside and across the street to a drugstore, where Jack treated the others to hot chocolate soda.

"They are hatching out something, that is sure," remarked Jack.

"As near as I could make out, Werner is going off into the woods on a hunt and wants Glutts to go with him," returned Fred. "I wonder where they are going?"

No one could answer that question, and presently the crowd began to talk of other things, and especially of the war play they had just witnessed.

"Gosh! but a play like that brings the war pretty close to a fellow," said Randy, with a sigh.

"Makes a fellow think of how our dads are making out over there, doesn't it?" said Fred.

"When they showed those ambulance scenes with all the dead and dying lying around it gave me the cold shivers," came from Andy. "I tell you what—war is a terrible thing."

"Yes, and you have got to see something like that to realize how really terrible it is," put in Jack.

Several days later the term at Colby Hall came to an end. There was something of an entertainment, with prize speaking in which Spouter distinguished himself, and then came the final drill and parade around the campus. Following this the cadets indulged in several snowball fights and in quite some horseplay, and then rushed off to their rooms to pack their suitcases and other baggage so as to be ready to depart for home in the early morning.

"Wow! but it feels good to know I haven't got to look at a grammar or an algebra for the next few weeks," cried Randy, with satisfaction.

"Say! it makes me feel as happy as a clown in a circus," declared Andy, and, in high spirits, he began a jig and ended by turning a flip-flap over one of the beds. Then he and his twin indulged in a pillow fight, in which Fred joined.

"Hi, you fellows! stop your rumpus," cried Jack, who was trying to pack his suitcase. "You keep on, and you'll have the ceiling of the floor below down."

"Can't help it!" cried Andy gayly. "We've got to break loose once in a while," and he playfully landed a cake of soap in the open suitcase.

"I'll soap you!" cried the young captain, and, taking the article in question, he made a leap over the bed, caught his cousin by the neck, and allowed the cake of soap to slip down Andy's back.

"Great salt mackerel!" ejaculated the fun-loving Rover, and, pulling his coat tight, he arched his back. "Anybody notice the camel's hump?"

"It isn't a hump, Andy. It's only a wart on your backbone," answered his twin.

"Well, hump or wart, it isn't going to stay there very long," remarked the other, and immediately proceeded to stand on his hands, shaking his body in such a manner that presently the soap rattled out on the floor. Then quietness was restored for the time being, and the Rovers continued their packing.

A conference was held with Gif, and it was decided that all of the crowd were to go home for Christmas. Several days later the Rovers were to meet Gif and Spouter at Portview, and then all would proceed to Cedar Lodge.

"And don't forget to bring your guns and all your other traps," said Gif.

"You trust us for that!" responded Fred.

"We'll be there with everything that is necessary outside of the provisions. Those, of course, we can get at Portview or at Timminsport."

"I hope we get a chance at a moose," sighed Randy.

"Gee! Why don't you make it a lion or an elephant or a polar bear while you are at it?" cried his twin. "Might as well wish for everything in the menagerie. It doesn't cost any more," and at this there was a general smile.

"I know what I'd like to get," said Jack. "I was reading about one in the paper the other day. They must be beautiful creatures."

"What's that?" questioned Gif.

"A silver fox."

"Oh, say, Jack! that would be fine. But I imagine silver foxes are exceedingly rare."

"Oh, I know that. Just the same, I'd like to bag one. The fur would make a very fine piece for some lady to wear."

"Ruth Stevenson, for instance," murmured Andy; and at this his cousin made a playful pass at him with his fist, which the fun-loving Rover easily dodged.

The next morning the cadets had an early breakfast, and a short while later saw many of them on their way by carriage and automobile to Haven Point. Many girls were also coming in from Clearwater Hall, so that the railroad station present an unusually lively appearance.

In the crowd was Bill Glutts, but he took care to keep away from the Rovers. Gabe Werner was nowhere to be seen, and the Rovers rightfully conjectured that he had left the town.

The boys had hardly arrived when a carry-all came in from Clearwater Hall containing Mary and Martha, as well as Ruth and May and a dozen other girl students. There was a general handshaking, and then all took a stand on the station platform to wait for the coming of two trains which were to bear the various students in opposite directions. Everybody had already procured a ticket, and the trains which were expected were extras, for it would have been impossible for the ordinary locals to have taken care of such heavy traffic.

"I am sorry you're not going to travel with us to New York," said Jack to Ruth.

"Well, I'm sorry you're not coming my way," answered the girl, with a smile.

"But you'll be down to our house directly after Christmas,

won't you?"

"Yes, we'll be down the day after—May and I."

"Well, that will give us a whole day together, anyhow, before us fellows start for Cedar Lodge," went on the young captain. Then he nudged Ruth in the elbow. "Come over here," he whispered. "I want to show you something that I don't want the others to see."

Together they slipped out of the crowd and around the corner of the little railroad station. Then Jack brought out a large flat package from an inner pocket of his overcoat. "I had these taken as a Christmas surprise to mother and Martha. What do you think of them?" and he brought forth several photographs of himself taken in his cadet uniform. They had been taken by the leading photographer of Haven Point who made a specialty of work for the two schools, and they certainly showed the young captain at his best.

"Oh, how lovely, Jack!" cried Ruth in genuine pleasure. "I declare, they are splendid pictures."

"Then you like them?" he queried anxiously.

"I certainly do! I don't think they could be better." She looked at the three poses presented critically. "If it's all the same to you, I'll keep this one," she said finally.

"Oh, Ruth, you don't want my picture, do you?" he questioned, and there was a trace of wistfulness in his voice.

"Of course I do, Jack. I can keep this one, can't I?" and the girl looked full at him in a manner that spoke volumes.

"Why, sure! if you want it," he answered quickly. "But, say!

Arthur M. Winfield

don't I get one of yours in return?" he added.

"Well, I'll see about that," she hesitated.

"Oh, now, Ruth—"

"I haven't had one taken in an awfully long time, Jack."

"Never mind, you will let me have one of them anyhow, won't you?"

"I—I guess—maybe so. I'll give it to you for a Christmas present. Only don't tell the others."

"I won't, Ruth. And you can keep about my picture to yourself, too," added the captain. And thereupon the decidedly interesting conversation between the pair had to come to an end as one of the trains came puffing in—that which was to carry Ruth and some of the other girls, as well as many of the cadets, away.

CHAPTER VIII

CHRISTMAS AT HOME

"Well, here we are at last. I wonder if anybody will be at the station to meet us," said Martha Rover.

"Oh, I'm sure somebody will come down," answered Mary.

The six Rovers had had a long and uneventful train ride from Haven Point to the Grand Central Terminal, Forty-second Street, New York City. They had had to change cars at the Junction, where some months before they had had such fun with Mr. Asa Lemm, the discharged teacher of the Hall, as related in detail in the volume previous to this. The train had been crowded with passengers, but the Rovers had managed to get seats together, much to their satisfaction; and they had also managed to get pretty fair accommodations when it came time to go into the diner.

They had telegraphed ahead concerning their coming, and found two chauffeurs employed by Dick Rover and Tom Rover on hand to receive them and take charge of their baggage. Then they went out to the street, where they found two automobiles awaiting them, one containing Jack's mother and the other the mothers of Fred and the twins.

Arthur M. Winfield

"Hello, Ma!" cried the young captain, as he rushed forward to embrace his parent. "How are you? You are looking pretty good."

"Oh, I am feeling quite fair," answered Mrs. Dick Rover with a smile.

"Home again, and glad of it!" exclaimed Fred, as he embraced his mother.

"My, my, but I'm glad that that term at the school is at an end!" cried Andy, as he gave Mrs. Tom Rover the hug he knew she would be expecting, a hug which was speedily duplicated by his twin. "Hope you've got a good big dinner waiting for us. Traveling has made me hungry."

"Not but what we had a pretty good meal on the train," added his twin.

"You'll get all you want to-night," answered Mrs. Tom Rover affectionately.

In the meantime Mary and Martha had come up and joined their parents. There was a good deal of kissing and questioning, and while this was going on the chauffeurs assisted the young people to their seats and stowed away their handbaggage. There were no trunks to come, for all the young folks had left a large part of the belongings at the schools.

There was only one thing which saddened the home-coming of the young people, and that was the absence of their fathers. Although Jack had said that his mother was looking well, still he had not failed to notice that her face showed a certain paleness and some lines of care.

"Don't worry, Mother. I'm sure dad will come back all right," he said later on, in an endeavor to comfort her.

"I am hoping so, Jack. But, oh! how I wish this awful war would come to an end," and Mrs. Dick Rover sighed deeply.

All too quickly the next few days passed. Young folks and old folks were busy doing their shopping for Christmas, and in addition to this, the boys went out to purchase a number of things they thought they might need while at the camp.

"I'm afraid we're in for it," said Randy dismally, on the afternoon before Christmas. "This looks like a regular blizzard."

It certainly did look like a blizzard, with the snow coming down thickly and the wind blowing it first in one direction then in another. By nightfall the streets were almost impassable, and in the morning traffic along Riverside Drive was practically suspended.

"Merry Christmas!" shouted Randy, who was the first to get up.

"Merry Christmas!" replied Andy. "And how do you like to live at the North Pole?" he added, as he glanced out of the window at the storm-bound street and the river and the Palisades beyond.

There was a grand reunion of the three families in the Dick Rover residence, and presents were exchanged all around. The boys had purchased a number of small but appropriate gifts for their mothers and the two girls, and also for the various servants of the families. In return they received a number of gifts, both useful and ornamental, including gold-mounted stylographic pens, which each one had desired, and also some new hockey skates and story books.

Martha had knit a bright sweater for her brother, and Mary had done the same for Fred, and the girls between them had likewise knit sweaters for the twins.

"We sure are the lucky kids," remarked Andy, when all of them were looking over their gifts. "This sweater suits me to a T. And, my! just wait until I get on those hockey skates. There won't be a thing in New York or on Clearwater Lake that will beat me."

"I see you doing some tall skating to-day," replied his twin, with a grin. "What you will need is a snow shovel if you want to get anywhere."

The storm kept up until noon of Christmas, and then cleared away almost as rapidly as it had come, the night being clear and cold, with a beautiful moon and twinkling stars shining from above.

"I hope it stays clear so that May and Ruth will have a chance to come down," remarked Fred during the course of the afternoon.

"I guess we all hope that," answered Jack.

With so much to think of in connection with their proposed trip to Cedar Lodge, the Rover boys put in a busy time all of that day and part of the next. Then they went down to the Grand Central Terminal with the girls to meet the expected visitors.

"There they are!" cried Martha, after the long train had rolled into the station. And a moment later she and Ruth were in each other's arms, while Mary was embracing May. Then the boys shook hands, and all drove away to the Rover residences.

"Did you get that picture for me, Ruth?" questioned Jack, as soon as he could get a chance to speak to the girl in private.

"Oh, you don't want any picture," she declared mischievously.

"Aw, come now," he pleaded, "don't try to put me off that way. You know what you promised."

"Well, can't you wait until we get to the house?"

"Oh, sure! But I wanted to make certain that you had brought the picture along."

"You'll be scared when you see it," declared Ruth. "I look a perfect fright. The man snapped the picture before I was half ready."

But later on, when Jack received the gift, he declared that the picture was a very good one indeed, although it did not look half as pretty as Ruth did herself. The two had quite a little fun over the picture, and then Jack placed it in his pocket.

"Now you've got it, what are you going to do with it?" questioned Ruth curiously.

"I'm going to carry it right here," he declared, for he had it in an inside pocket over his heart.

"Oh, you big goose!" cried Ruth, but then she blushed and looked pleased nevertheless.

It was announced that part of the lake in Central Park had

been scraped clear of the snow, and the following day the young folks went skating and had a most glorious time. Then in the evening all attended a theatrical performance at one of the leading theaters.

"Oh, my! but I am having a splendid time," said Ruth to Martha.

"It's too bad the boys are going away," was the answer. "But I don't blame them for wanting to go on a hunt. If I were a boy I'd like to go on a hunt myself."

On the following morning came a letter from Dick Rover, stating that matters were still somewhat quiet in the sector in France where they were located, but that word was being passed around that they were to make an advance in the near future.

"Hurrah! I guess they'll show those Huns what Americans can do," cried Jack.

"Oh, I dread to think of their going into battle!" said his mother.

"Ma, while we are away don't forget to send us any news that may come in," said Jack quickly. "You can telegraph to Timminsport, and we will leave word there at the telegraph office so that any important message will be delivered to us."

"I'll certainly do that, Jack." And later on Mrs. Tom Rover and Mrs. Sam Rover promised to do the same thing.

"There is no telling what may happen to our dads if they get into a regular first-class battle," remarked Fred, that night when the four boys were holding a little conference among themselves.

"Well, we've got to take what comes," returned Randy briefly. "However, I'll be as much worried as ma until this war is at an end or until our dads come home."

The boys had looked over their traps with care and examined their rifles and shotguns, and had even gone down into the cellar of one of their residences to try out the weapons to make certain that they were in working order.

With a shotgun in his hand Andy wanted to have some fun with one of the servant girls, but Randy quickly stopped him.

"Nothing doing, Andy," he said. "You'll only make ma nervous, and she is nervous enough already, thinking about dad. You save your tomfoolery until we are on the way or up at the camp."

At length came the time for the boys to take their departure. Jack hated to think of running away from Ruth, and Fred was equally sorry to leave May Powell behind, yet the thought of what was ahead brightened all of the lads considerably.

"We ought to have the time of our lives," declared Fred. "That is, if hunting is half as good as Gif Garrison said it was."

"And if I can get that silver fox," added Jack.

"Nothing but a moose for me," declared Randy. "Either a moose or a six-legged jack rabbit."

"Wouldn't you like to shoot a bear that weighed about a thousand pounds?" questioned Jack.

"And lug the carcass to camp yourself?" came from Fred.

"Speaking about carrying a thousand-pound bear puts me in mind of something," cried Randy quickly. "A fellow was telling me of a man here in the city who carried twelve hundred pounds."

"Twelve hundred pounds!" exclaimed his twin. "It can't be done."

"Why, that's more than a half a ton!" said Jack incredulously.

"Never mind, the fellow carried the twelve hundred pounds," went on Randy. "A whole lot of people saw him do it."

"Where was this?" questioned Fred.

"It was down at one of the Broadway banks," answered Randy innocently. "The fellow was an English army officer. He had twelve hundred pounds in English money that he was exchanging for good old U. S. A. coin."

"Fooled!" cried Fred, and this was followed by a general laugh.

CHAPTER IX

THE RAILROAD ACCIDENT

The four Rover boys journeyed from New York City to Baxton and there changed from one station to another nearby and took the next train for Portview.

Arriving in Portview they took a taxicab to the leading hotel, and were there met by Gif and Spouter, who had come in a few hours earlier and had already signed for their accommodations.

"Mighty glad to see you got here," declared Gif. "I read about the awful storm you had down around New York, and I thought you might be delayed."

"Well, I see they have had some of the snow up here," answered Jack. "Although it isn't as heavy as it was down our way."

"Don't worry about snow, Jack. You'll get all you want of it after we reach Cedar Lodge."

The Rover boys were tired out from their all-day trip, and as Gif and Spouter had likewise had their fill of traveling for the time being, all were glad enough to retire for a good

Arthur M. Winfield

night's rest, even Andy being too worn out to play any of his jokes. But the following morning found the youths as bright and fresh as ever and eager to continue their journey.

"We can get a train for Timminsport at ten-thirty," announced Gif. "That will give us plenty of time for breakfast and to do a little shopping if we need anything. Portview has as good stores as many big towns. When you get to Timminsport, you will find it nothing but a one-horse country town."

They had a substantial breakfast, and then wandered down the main street as far as a small park, and then came back on the other side of the thoroughfare. They made a number of small purchases, including some cakes of choice chocolate and a bag of almonds, of which Spouter and Randy were particularly fond.

"When we get to Timminsport don't forget to add a good big bag of sugar to our stores," said Randy. "Then, if we are snowed in sometime, we can spend a few hours making some home-made candy."

"Yes, and we can try our hands at some cookies," added Fred. "I've watched our cook make them quite a few times, and I think I could make some myself if I tried real hard."

"Anyway, you might be able to turn out some sinkers," said Andy, with a grin. "And if we couldn't eat 'em we could take 'em back to Colby Hall and present 'em to some of the teachers for paperweights." And at this there was a laugh.

With the bundles the boys returned to the hotel, paid their bill, and with their suitcases in hand, returned once more to the depot. Here in the smoky trainshed the cars were already waiting, and they climbed aboard; and a few minutes later were on their way to Timminsport.

The coast in this vicinity is very irregular, so that the train did not run close to the shore. They skirted a bay, and then branched off at a small place called Leeways for the town for which they were bound. At Leeways they met several heavy lumber trains, and also met a gang of men bound for one of the lumber camps.

"We are certainly getting away from the big towns now," remarked Fred.

"I just saw a few hunters with their guns!" cried Randy. "That looks interesting to me!"

There was no diner on the train, but around noon it stopped at a way-station where there was a lunch counter, and here the young travelers had ten minutes in which to satisfy their appetites.

"Maybe we'd better take a few sandwiches along," remarked Jack. "We may not have another chance to eat until we get to the Lodge."

"Oh, there is a little restaurant at Timminsport," declared Gif. "It's not a very nice place, but we'll be able to get as much as we want there."

Soon the train was on its way again, having backed up at Leeways to drop a passenger car and take on one of mixed freight. The character of the passengers had largely changed, and most of them were now country folks, lumberjacks, and city people bound for a season of hunting. The steam heat had died out in the car which the boys occupied, and it was growing colder and colder.

"The train doesn't go any farther than Timminsport," explained Gif, "and I suppose the engineer is saving on steam."

"Say, Gif, I didn't think you were going to give us such a cold reception!" cried Randy.

"Never mind the cold reception!" exclaimed Spouter, who was gazing out of the window at the scenery. "Just look at this truly wonderful picture! See those hillsides with massive pines, and those clusters of bushes, all bent down with their weight of snow. And see how the sunshine sparkles, making each snowdrop look like a diamond. It's a wonderful sight, and it fills one's soul with a feeling of awe and admiration for—"

"Hurrah! Spouter has come into his own again," cried Andy. "That's right, Spout, warm up good, and maybe you'll help warm this car."

"If those snowdrops were really diamonds, Spouter, what do you thing they'd be worth a dozen?" came from Randy.

"Aw, that's just like you fellows!" grumbled the would-be orator, in disgust. "You haven't any poetry in your souls."

"Haven't any poetry in my soul?" cried Andy. "You bet I have—tons and tons of it! Just listen to this," and he chanted gayly:

"I love to see a snowdrop
    Ahanging on a tree,
Aglistening in the sunshine
    As happy as can be."

"Great red-headed snakes!" burst out Jack. "Andy has turned poet!"

"Don't you think you ought to take something for it, Andy? Cough mixture, or measles eradicator, or something like that?" questioned Fred.

"I think what he needs is a good dose of codliver oil, served hot," came from Gif.

"No codliver oil for me!" cried the fun-loving Rover. "You deal that out to Spouter. It will help oil his tongue and make his flow of oratory better."

"Speaking of cough mixtures, I think I'll get a bottle of some sort when we get to Timminsport if they have a drugstore," said Jack. "Some of us may catch cold and need it."

With such talk going on, the journey continued. They were now running for a small station named Enwood, where they were to pick up two extra cars from a small side road coming down from the north. In this section there was a good deal of snow, and the train, consequently, had to run rather slowly.

"I think I could get out and walk almost as fast as this train is moving," remarked Spouter presently.

"It isn't as bad as that, Spouter," returned Jack, looking out of the window. "We are making at least fifteen miles an hour, and you couldn't hoof it as quick as that."

"It certainly seems awfully slow," remarked Fred. He was beginning to grow sleepy, and now he rested his head on the back of the seat and closed his eyes.

"Perhaps we won't be able to get through to Timminsport," came from Randy. "That would be a fine state of affairs, eh?"

Arthur M. Winfield

"I don't see any houses along the line. We'd have one sweet job finding a place to go to if the train became snowbound," said Andy.

"They generally manage to keep this road open, no matter how bad the storms are," declared Gif. "You see, the hunters are coming and going all the time, as well as the lumbermen and the folks that live in and around Timminsport and Enwood. They don't like to be cut off from the rest of the world, even for a day or two."

"I hope we don't have to wait for that other train when we get to Enwood," said Spouter. "That may be awfully late, you know."

"I asked the conductor awhile ago, and he said they hoped it would be on time. It comes down hill most of the way, and that is in its favor. If they had to pull uphill much, they might get stuck."

Presently they passed a small lumber camp, and one of the other passengers told the boys they were now within half a mile of Enwood.

"And that is only twelve miles from Timminsport," said Gif. "We ought to be there in about half an hour or so."

They had struck a portion of the track which was comparatively free of snow, and the engineer of the train was now trying to make up some of the lost time. The boys were congratulating themselves on this when they suddenly heard a shriek of the locomotive whistle, followed instantly by the sudden application of the steam brakes. The train shuddered and shook, and two seconds later there came a crash from the front, and then the train came to a sudden stop.

The Rover boys and their chums had leaped to their feet at the first shock. The second threw Spouter headlong, and Randy went down almost on top of him. Fred was awakened from his brief nap by having his forehead bumped upon the seat ahead of him.

"What's the matter?"

"What did we strike?"

"Are we going to upset?"

"Let me get out of here! I don't want to be smashed up!"

Such were some of the cries which rent the air while the train was still in motion and after it came to a standstill. Every passenger had been shaken up, and not a few were knocked down. Fortunately, however, no one in that particular car seemed to be much hurt, although several were bruised and every one was more or less nervous.

"Are you hurt, Fred?" questioned Jack quickly, as he saw his young cousin feeling of his forehead.

"Well, I got a pretty good bump," answered the youngest Rover, "and I guess I'm going to have a lump there as a consequence."

"We'll get out and see what's doing, and then you can put some snow on it."

Some of the passengers were already leaving the car, and the Rover boys and their chums quickly followed. The trouble was all ahead, and they had some difficulty in wading through the snow alongside the track to get to the front of the train.

Arthur M. Winfield

Here it was plain to be seen what had happened. The train from the north had come in and tried to take the siding, as was the custom. But the switch had become blocked with snow, and the train had been thrown out on the main track, which at this point, crossed the track on which the train from Portview was coming. The big locomotive of the latter train had ploughed through the middle of the train from the north, hitting the latter between two of the cars and sending those cars in either direction to the sides of the track.

"Gee! this is some wreck!" exclaimed Gif.

"I should say it was!" declared Jack. "It looks to me as if somebody might be killed."

From the two wrecked cars came cries of pain and yells for help. One of the cars still stood up, but at a dangerous angle, while the other had turned completely over and rested on its top in the snow.

All was excitement, and for the time being everyone seemed to be so dazed that but little was done. Passengers were leaping from both of the wrecked cars, some coming through the doorways and some through the broken-out windows. Jack and Randy ran to one of the cars, and were able to assist a woman with a little girl to alight and reach a place of safety. In the meanwhile, the other lads assisted two elderly men. One had his foot hurt, and they carried him into the railroad station, where they laid him on one of the benches.

"Look! Look!" cried Fred suddenly, forgetting all about his hurt forehead. "Look! That car over yonder is on fire!"

The car he mentioned was that which had turned over and was resting on its top in the snow. From the interior thick black smoke was coming, and this was presently followed by a tongue of flame. The car was a combination baggage and smoker, and it was afterwards learned that one of the passengers had been carrying a can of kerosene which had broken open in the smash-up, and had evidently become ignited by some thrown-down cigar or cigarette.

"Those people will be in danger of burning up!" gasped Randy.

"They will be unless they get out in a hurry," answered Spouter.

From the interior of the car came more cries, and presently all outside heard a man yelling in a tone of agony:

"Help! Help! Somebody save me! My leg is caught fast, and I can't get out! Save me!"

Arthur M. Winfield

CHAPTER X

THE RESCUE

"There's a man left in there!"

"He says his leg is caught fast!"

"Help! Help!" came more faintly from the interior of the burning car. "Help, or I'll be burnt to death!"

Only a few passengers seemed to hear these cries, for most of the men who had come from the other train were gathered near the car which was still standing. The Rover boys and their chums listened in horror to the call for assistance. Jack was the first to leap forward.

"We'll have to save that fellow if we can," he cried determinedly.

"I think he is close to one of these windows," said Randy, pointing to several broken-out windows through which some other passengers in the car had climbed.

"Wait! I've got an idea!" exclaimed Fred. "See that stick of wood? Why can't we place that against one of the windows and climb up on it?"

He had pointed to a plank one end of which, in some manner, had become torn up from the roadbed. All of the boys rushed for this plank and turned and twisted it until they had the fastened end under the snow loose. Then they rushed over to the burning car and placed the plank on a slant from the snow to the broken-out window which, because the overturned car was not on a level, was two or three feet above their heads.

Jack was the first to get on the plank, and speedily crawled up to the window. Fortunately a draft was taking most of the smoke to the other side of the car, so that he could see into the interior quite plainly.

A scene of great confusion met the eyes of the young captain. A number of broken seats had fallen down on the ceiling of the car and in the midst of this wreckage lay a short, stocky man with several cuts and bruises on his face from which the blood was flowing. The man had his arms and one leg free, but several seats and some handbaggage were wedged in across his left leg and his stomach in such a manner that he seemed unable to extricate himself. The fire was creeping up to within a few inches of his caught foot, and this had caused him to raise his wild cry for assistance.

"Help! Help!" he repeated, as soon as he caught sight of Jack's face framed in the broken-out window. "Get me out of here before the fire reaches me!"

"We'll do it!" answered Jack. "Come on, Randy. I think the two of us can do the trick," he added to his cousin, who had come up behind him on the plank.

"Want any more help?" questioned the others simultaneously.

Arthur M. Winfield

"If we do we'll let you know quick enough."

Jack dropped down into the car, and Randy followed. They landed among a mass of broken glass and other wreckage, but to this paid no attention.

"Here, Randy, take hold of this seat and pull it back," ordered Jack; and between them they set to work with vigor.

But it was no mean task to get all of the wreckage off of the trapped passenger. There were half a dozen heavy suitcases among the broken seats, and these the boys hurled through the broken windows, where they were picked up by those outside and carried to a safe place. In the meanwhile the flames were creeping closer, and now a sudden change in the air caused a heavy volume of smoke to drift toward them.

"Gee! this is getting fierce," spluttered Randy, and began to cough, while the tears started from his eyes.

"Don't leave me! Please don't leave me!" pleaded the passenger under the wreckage. "I don't want to be burnt up!" and then he said something in a foreign tongue which the others did not understand.

The last bit of wreckage was the hardest of all to get away from where it rested across the man's stomach. This was wedged in between the ceiling and the side of the car, and the boys had to use all their strength before they could dislodge it. But at last it came loose, and then the man was able to sit up.

"Here, we'll help you," cried Jack, as the passenger seemed to be too weak to regain his feet. He and Randy caught the fellow under his arms and, standing him upright, dragged him to the window upon which the end of the plank rested.

They shoved him out, and he went rolling and sliding down the plank into the snow. Randy followed him quickly, and then came Jack.

The rescue had occurred none too soon, for the wind was now coming up, and soon the overturned car was a mass of smoke and flames from end to end. The boys left the plank where it was, and assisted the rescued passenger to the little railroad station, where all the others who had been injured had already been taken.

The short, stocky man was very much excited and he thanked the lads over and over again for what they had done.

"I wish I was a rich man," he said sadly, and now they noticed that he spoke with a decided accent. "If I was rich I would pay all of you well for what you have done. It was very noble—very noble indeed! I shall never forget it."

"We don't want any reward," answered Jack.

"You young gentlemen do not look as if you needed any reward," said the man, with a little smile, as he noted how well dressed the youths were. "I am a poor man, so I can offer you nothing but my thanks, but those I give you with all my heart. And now may I ask your names?"

They told him, and all shook hands. He said his name was Herman Crouse, and that he was a farmer working a small place some miles away. He was plainly dressed and evidently far from wealthy.

While the boys were assisting Herman Crouse to the little railroad station, others had gone into the burning car and picked up such baggage and other things as could be gotten out. Then the car, which was nothing but an old rattletrap

Arthur M. Winfield

affair, was allowed to burn up.

Of course the accident had caused a great deal of excitement, and telegrams were at once dispatched to Leeways and Timminsport for assistance.

"I think I'll send word home that we are all right," said Jack. "The folks may hear about this accident and worry over it," and as soon as he had an opportunity he sent a message, and Gif and Spouter did the same.

As the trains from the north ran no farther on that branch than Enwood, all of the passengers on board had been bound for either that place or Timminsport. Consequently many of those who were injured remained in the town, while the others were made as comfortable as possible on the other train and taken to Timminsport. Fortunately, no one had been killed or fatally hurt. Herman Crouse remained at Enwood. He thanked the boys again most heartily when they left him.

"Maybe some day I shall be able to pay you back for your goodness to me," said he. "If it comes that way, I shall certainly do it," and then he shook hands once more.

"I guess he's a German all right enough," remarked Jack, when the boys were once again in the train and it was moving forward, the track having been cleared. "He spoke with a very strong German accent."

"Yes, and his name is undoubtedly German," said Randy. "But he was a pretty decent sort, anyway."

"Oh, a good many of the German-Americans, so-called, are all right," said Gif. "Why, there are thousands of them in the army and in the navy, as well as in the air service. And they are fighting just as hard and loyally for Uncle Sam as anybody."

"Sure!" declared Andy. "Look at Hans Mueller, who used to be a great chum of our dads at Putnam Hall. He's as loyal as they make 'em, and he's in the army too, and will undoubtedly give a good account of himself."

"Oh, I don't doubt but what a lot of the Germans are loyal to this country," came from Spouter. "Just the same, it's a good thing to keep your eyes on them."

"Right you are!" cried Andy. "Don't forget those German spies we ran into at the offices in Wall Street—the same chaps who were in with Mr. Brown and Mr. Martell."

"I tell you one thing," remarked Gif, changing the subject. "This accident is going to get us into Timminsport very late, and I don't know whether Jed Wallop will be there to meet us or not." They had sent word ahead for the old fellow who lived near the Cedar Lodge property to come with his boxsled for them and their traps.

"Probably he was hanging around the railroad station waiting for the train to come in, and, if so, he must have heard about the accident, and he would be very anxious about you, Gif," remarked Jack.

"Well, we'll see when we get there. But if Jed isn't there, I don't know what we can do for the night. I don't believe Timminsport has any hotel fit to stop at, and it wouldn't be a very nice hike of five or six miles to Cedar Lodge in the dark and through the snow."

With so many hurt passengers on board, the engineer was careful, and so did not run very fast, and as a consequence it was well after dark by the time they rolled into Timminsport. Quite a crowd was collected at the depot, anxious to get the particulars of the accident, and also to meet those who needed assistance. The two doctors living in that vicinity had been summoned and were on hand to give all the aid possible.

"There is Jed Wallop now!" cried Gif presently, and pointed to a tall, angular individual wrapped up in a shaggy overcoat and wearing an equally shaggy cap with the eartabs tied down under his chin.

"Hello, Jed!" he cried cheerfully, and shoved his way forward to greet the man.

Jed Wallop proved to be so excited that he hardly paid attention to Gif's greetings nor to his introduction to the other youths from Colby Hall.

"I'm lookin' fer a cousin o' mine—Tim Doolittle," he exclaimed. "I heard as how he was in the accident. Did you see him?"

"I don't know the man, Jed," answered Gif. "The hurt ones are all in the forward car."

Jed Wallop pushed his way through the crowd and soon found the man he was seeking. The poor fellow had one arm in a sling and had several cuts on his face, and declared himself very much "shook up" and rather weak.

"Well, by gosh! I'm mighty glad you wasn't killed, Tim," declared Wallop. "Now, what you goin' to do with yourself? You can't go up to Burke's Camp in that condition."

"No, I can't," answered Tim Doolittle. "I've got to rest up fer a spell and git this sprained arm o' mine fit fer work agin. I was thinkin' I might ride over to Uncle Joe's place if I could git anyone to take me."

"I can take you there myself. I can git a sleigh from Hank Miller and do it—that is, if these young fellers would be willin' to drive over to Cedar Lodge alone," added Jed Wallop, looking anxiously at Gif and his companions.

"I suppose I could do that," answered Gif slowly. "I don't know the way very well, but I think I could make it."

"Oh, it's a putty straight road, Gif," said Wallop. "You can't miss your way if you keep your eyes open. Whenever you strike the crossroads keep to the right every time, and then you won't git left," and he chuckled a little over his joke.

"How are the team and the boxsled?"

"All right. You know them horses—Mary and John, a very reliable team. They won't run away, and they'll make good time."

"All right then, Jed. Just show me where the sled is, and then you can go off and take care of your cousin," said Gif. "We'll have to stay in town for a while and see if we can't pick up some grub and at least enough supplies to last us for a few days."

So the matter was arranged, and a few minutes later Jed Wallop went off to see what he could do about caring for his injured cousin.

"It's all right for him to look after his cousin," remarked Gif. "But that leaves us to go on alone. I hope we find everything at Cedar Lodge all right."

"Oh, it will be a lark to go on all alone!" cried Fred. "We don't want that fellow along. We can get along alone very well."

Arthur M. Winfield

"I know what I want to do first of all," declared Andy. "I want to get a bite to eat. That sandwich I had didn't satisfy me at all."

"All right, we'll go to that restaurant I spoke about," said Gif. "Then we'll get our provisions and be on the way to the Lodge."

CHAPTER XI

ON THE WAY TO CEDAR LODGE

The restaurant Gif had in mind was a small affair located on a side street directly behind the railroad station. Leaving their handbaggage at the station in a pile with numerous other bags, and their guns with the station-master, they made their way to this resort. Ordinarily at this time of night the restaurant was doing very little business, but on account of the accident many people had dropped in, so the tables presented a lively appearance.

"We'll have some difficulty in finding seats, I guess," remarked Jack, looking around.

"There are a couple of small tables over in the alcove," came from Spouter. "We might shove them together, and I guess they'll hold us all."

This was done, and after a wait of several minutes a girl came to take their orders.

"What have you got ready?" questioned Gif. "There is no use of our waiting to have anything cooked to order," he continued to his chums.

Arthur M. Winfield

The girl named over a variety of things, including hot pork and beans, roast beef with potatoes and turnips, and also several kinds of sandwiches and pies, and also tea and coffee.

"Those things will do first rate, I guess," cried Fred. "Me for a dish of pork and beans and a good hot cup of coffee!"

It did not take the cadets long to give their orders, and the girl bustled off to serve them. While the lads were waiting for the things to be brought, Andy happened to glance across the restaurant at the other patrons and suddenly gave a low whistle of surprise.

"Look who's here, will you!" he exclaimed.

All looked in the direction pointed out, and there, at a side table, saw Bill Glutts, Gabe Werner and Henry Stowell.

"My gracious! what do you know about that?" ejaculated Randy. "Glutts, Werner and Codfish!"

"What can those fellows be doing in Timminsport?" demanded Spouter.

"Say! I think I know the answer to that question," returned Jack quickly. He looked at his cousin Fred. "Don't you remember what Bill and Gabe said in the moving picture theater about going up to some camp to hunt? I wager that camp is located somewhere in this vicinity."

"That must be it!" answered Fred.

"However did they get poor Codfish to come along with them?" queried Andy. "They'll plague the life out of that little sneak."

"They'll make a regular servant of him, that's what they'll do!" answered his twin.

"If they came up here to hunt, I hope they are not going to settle down anywhere near Cedar Lodge," remarked Gif. "I'd hate to have those fellows saddled on me while I was trying to have some fun."

"I wonder if they saw us?" questioned Fred.

"Let's not take any notice of them," advised Jack. "I'd rather go my way and let them go theirs."

To this the others readily agreed. They were soon served with the things they had ordered and lost no time in making away with the food. Then they hurried out of the resort, leaving Glutts, Werner and Codfish still at the table which they occupied. The two bullies had lighted cigarettes.

"Now let's skip over to one of the general stores and see what we can get in the way of provisions," said Gif. "We'll have to hurry up, or the storekeeper may close up on us."

"I've got the list here, Gif," declared Jack. "Show us where the store is, and then you bring around the team with the boxsled. By that time maybe we'll have most of our things bought."

The store proved to be a low, rambling affair filled with a hundred and one varieties of goods, some looking quite fresh and others with the appearance of having been in stock for some years.

The storekeeper was pleased to serve them, especially when he realized that their purchases would be for cash. Jack and the others knew exactly what they wanted, and picked out everything with care.

"I guess you young fellows have been up in the woods before," remarked the storekeeper, with a shrewd look.

"We have been, although not around here," answered Jack.

"Thought you had by the way you're ordering. Some of them fellows that come up here have no more idee about what is wanted in a camp than nothing at all. They take along the most ridiculous things, and sometimes leave out coffee and sugar and salt and bacon and things like that which a feller has jest got to have."

Gif had brought around the boxsled, and into this the storekeeper's assistant piled the various boxes and bags which contained the provisions they had purchased. The things made quite a load, so that the six cadets had about all they could do to get in themselves.

"We sure would have been crowded had Jed Wallop been along," remarked Fred, who was squeezed in on top of some boxes with Randy on one side of him and Spouter on the other. Gif was up in front driving, with Jack and Andy beside him.

"Let her go!" cried Andy gayly. "Hurrah for Cedar Lodge!"

"Hold on!" exclaimed Jack suddenly. "Are you fellows going up there without your suitcases and guns?"

At this there came a groan from nearly all of the others.

"Gee! I forgot all about those suitcases and firearms."

"Where in the world are we going to place them?"

"If we put the suitcases in, we'll surely have to walk!"

"Oh, we'll stow 'em in somehow," declared Gif. "You fellows don't know how to load a boxsled."

"I know what we can do!" cried Jack. "Let us get a few loose packing-case boards and stand them up around the back of the sled. We can place the boxes against them, and then pile the suitcases on top, and the tops of the boards will hold them in. The guns can go in anywhere."

"That's the stuff!" said Spouter and he and Gif and Andy hurried back to the store to get the boards and arrange them as suggested.

In the meantime, Jack, Fred and Randy hurried in the direction of the railroad station to get the six suitcases and the guns which had been left there. They found the crowd had thinned out somewhat, although quite a few people were still present.

It did not take the three lads long to find the six suitcases, and, armed with two each and with all the guns, they trudged back to where they had left the boxsled. Then the suitcases were piled up and tied fast to the upright boards and to the boxsled itself, so that they might not be jounced off. The guns were placed in the bottom alongside the boxes.

"Now then, pile in, and we'll be getting to the Lodge," cried Gif. "I can tell you fellows I am mighty anxious to see the old place, to see if it looks like it did when I was here last."

The youths were just stowing themselves away on the sled when there came a cry from out of the darkness, and three fellows came hurrying through the snow from the direction of the railroad station.

"Hi, there! Stop!" called out the foremost of the trio. "Stop, I tell you!"

"Why, it's Gabe Werner!" exclaimed Randy. "What can he want of us?"

In a moment more the big bully was beside the sled, and Glutts and Codfish followed him.

"Thought you were mighty smart, eh?" cried Gabe Werner angrily. "Another minute, and I suppose you would have been gone!"

"What do you want, Werner?" demanded Jack.

"What are you fellows doing in this neighborhood?" questioned Fred.

"What we are doing here is our business," answered Werner sourly. "What I want of you is my suitcase."

"Your suitcase?" queried several of the others.

"Yes, my suitcase! Oh, you needn't play the innocent! I know you've got my suitcase somewhere on this boxsled. But you're not going to get away with it. Hand it over, or I'll call a policeman."

Gabe Werner was very much in earnest, and his face was red with anger and resentment. He reached up and caught hold of the lines which Gif held in his hands.

"Drop those lines, Werner!" cried Gif quickly. "Drop them, I say!"

"I want my suitcase! You had no business to touch it!"

"I don't know anything about your suitcase," declared Gif. He turned to the others. "We haven't anything but our own bags, have we?"

"I don't think we have," declared Jack.

"I know better!" grumbled Werner.

"I'll bet they've got it and are hiding it away," declared Bill Glutts. "They took a whole lot of bags away just as we were coming up. The baggage master saw 'em."

"I'm glad they didn't get my bag!" cried Codfish, who was lugging a good-sized Gladstone.

"If we took your bag it must have been by mistake," said Randy. "I looked at the markings pretty carefully though."

"So did I," said Fred.

"Well, we'll make sure," remarked Jack, and brought out a flashlight which he had taken from his own suitcase for possible use on the road. He flashed the light in the direction of the six suitcases, and he and his chums looked over all of the markings with care.

"How is your bag marked?" questioned Gif.

"G. A. W.," answered Werner.

"Well, you can see for yourself that there is no such marking on any of these bags," declared Jack. "There is my own. These two belong to Andy and Randy. This is Fred's, and here is Gif's and that one is Spouter's."

"Maybe they've got it hidden under the blankets, or

something like that," suggested Glutts.

"There are no other suitcases in this boxsled," declared Gif flatly.

"We'll take a look and make sure."

"You'll do nothing of the sort, Gabe Werner!" and now, with flashing eyes, Gif raised his whip as if to bring it down over the bully's head.

"Hold on, Gif! Don't do anything like that," advised Jack. "Let them look around the sled if they want to. Then they will know we're telling the truth. If we go off without giving them a chance to look, they may complain to the authorities here and make a lot of trouble for us."

"All right, then, go ahead and look," answered Gif, leaping from the boxsled. "But don't you harm any of our things, or you'll hear from me."

Jack flashed the light into the sled, and Werner and Glutts made an examination of the contents. Of course, they found no other baggage, and so drew back in disgust.

"I don't understand it," said Werner lamely. "I left that bag there in the station master's care while I and the others went to get something to eat. Now my bag is gone."

"Well, that is none of our affair," answered Jack. "Come on, fellows, it's getting late. Let's be on the way."

"I'll get that bag back, or I'll make the station master pay for it," grumbled Gabe Werner, and then he and his cronies turned on their heels and walked back in the direction of the railroad station.

"Gee! somebody must have walked off with his bag while he was eating," remarked Fred. "Rather tough luck if he had anything of real value in it."

"Serves him right—for being so cross and cranky," was Andy's comment. But the bag had not been stolen. It had been simply misplaced, as was afterwards proven.

Once more the boys adjusted themselves on the boxsled, and then Gif took up the reins and spoke to the team. Off they started at a walk, but soon broke into a slow trot as the sled began to go down a long slope leading in the direction of Cedar Lodge.

The way was little more than a woods road, winding in and out among the trees. They had to mount several small hills, and on these the horses settled down to a very slow walk.

"I guess Jed Wallop was right about Mary and John not running away," came from Randy. "I don't think anything short of an earthquake could start 'em into a gallop."

"They are lumber-camp horses, used to drawing pretty heavy loads," explained Gif. "They may not be very much on speed, but on the other hand you can depend on their pulling us out of any tight hole where fancy horses might get stuck."

　　　　Arthur M. Winfield

CHAPTER XII

AT THE FROZEN-UP SPRING

On and on went the boxsled carrying the Rovers and their chums, deeper and deeper into the woods. Occasionally the road was so narrow that they brushed the snow-laden bushes on one side or the other.

"Hi there, Gif, look out!" cried Randy presently. A bush had been turned aside by those ahead, and now it slipped back, covering Randy's face with loose snow.

"I'm sorry, Randy," returned Gif. "But we've got to take this road as it comes. You'll have to watch out, just as the others are doing."

There was a smoky lantern dangling from the front of the boxsled, but this gave little light. The moon was down beyond the trees, and only the diamond-like stars glittered overhead.

"How much further have we got to go?" questioned Jack presently, after they had passed a crossroads and kept to the right, as Jed Wallop had directed.

"I think we have covered about half the distance, Jack," was the reply of the young driver. "Still, I'm not sure. You know a boxsled isn't like an auto—it doesn't carry a speedometer."

"Gee! an auto would have been there and back two or three times since we started," was Fred's comment.

"Not in this snow," came from Spouter. "I think you'd get stuck in some of these deep places."

"They do use a few cars up here in the winter, but not many," said Gif. "It's too uncertain."

To make the time pass more quickly, Jack started one of the old school songs, and the others joined him. Then they ended with the well-known Colby Hall cry:

"Who are we?
Can't you see?
Colby Hall!
Dum! Dum! Dum, dum, dum!
Here we come with fife and drum!
Colby! Colby! Colby Hall!"

"I wonder what the neighbors will think if they hear us," remarked Randy.

"I don't think there are any neighbors very close," answered Gif. "There was a house some distance back, but I don't know of any others between here and Cedar Lodge. The other places are beyond the point where we turn off to go down to the bungalow."

They had now to make several sharp turns, and at these spots the road was unusually rough. One runner of the boxsled went up on some rocks, and for a moment it looked as if the turnout would upset.

"Look out there, Gif!"

"You'll have us in the snow with the sled on top of us!"

"Git along there, Mary and John!" cried the young driver. "Git along!" and he cracked his whip, and soon the team had pulled the boxsled from the rocks, and then going became better.

"We ought to be coming to a signboard soon," declared Gif a few minutes later. "I remember there used to be one on the road, pointing to a number of camps north of this place."

In a few minutes they came to the spot he had mentioned, but to his disappointment there was no signboard to be seen.

"Someone must have taken it down, or else it fell of itself," he remarked.

"Are you quite sure you're on the right road?" questioned Andy.

"It would be fierce to have to turn back this time of night," added his twin.

"Oh, I'm pretty sure this is the right road," answered their chum. Nevertheless, his face showed a doubtful look. Not to find the signboard which had been a landmark in that vicinity for many years puzzled him.

A little later they came to where the road branched out in three directions, the road on the right being narrow and running directly into a thick patch of woods.

"Whoa!" cried Gif to the team, and then he looked around more puzzled than ever, and shook his head.

"What's wrong now?" asked Jack.

"I guess I'm stumped," was the slow reply. "I can't remember this spot at all."

"Oh, Gif, don't tell us we're on the wrong road after all!" exclaimed Andy.

"Jed Wallop told us to keep to the right," announced Spouter. "We've been doing that, and we might as well do it now."

"But that road doesn't look as if it leads to anywhere," declared Fred.

"It's a mighty narrow road, too," returned Gif. "We might get down in among the trees and be unable to turn around, and then what would we do?"

"Better stay here, Gif, while I walk ahead and investigate," said Jack.

"Better take a gun along, in case you stir up something you don't want to meet," warned Fred.

"Not a bad idea," and, reaching down into the boxsled, Jack brought out one of the weapons that had been placed there.

"If you see a moose shoot him on the spot!" cried Randy.

"What spot?" queried his twin gayly. "A spot on the end of his tail or the tip of his ear wouldn't be of much account."

"I don't see how you can joke, Andy, when we're lost away out here in the woods and it's past midnight," came ruefully from Fred. "I'd give as much as a dollar to be at the Lodge and lying down in front of a roaring fire. I'm getting pretty cold."

Arthur M. Winfield

They were all cold, for since nightfall the thermometer had been going down steadily. More than this, the wind was rising, and this in the open places was anything but pleasant to the cadets.

"I'll go with you, Jack," announced Spouter, and he, too, armed himself with his gun, a double-barreled affair of which he was quite proud.

Holding his flashlight so that they might see where they were walking, Jack led the way, and Spouter came close behind. They walked a distance of several hundred feet, and here found that the road came to an end among some rocks which were now covered with ice.

"It's a road to a spring, that's all," said Jack. "The water is frozen now, but I suppose in the summer time the lumbermen and the other folks around here occasionally travel in for a drink. We may as well go back."

"Well, it's a mighty good thing we didn't drive in here. We might have had a job turning around on that rough ice," answered Spouter.

The frozen-up spring was a beautiful sight, the water standing out in columns and waves as if made of milky glass. Behind the columns there was still a trickle of water.

To get a better view of the sight, Jack swept the rays of the flashlight first to one side and then to the other. As he did this he caught a glimpse of a pair of gleaming eyes from the brushwood and snow behind the spring. The eyes looked full of curiosity and fright.

"Look, look, Spouter!" he cried, and then dropped the flashlight into his overcoat pocket.

"What is it?"

"I just saw the eyes of some wild animal back there. See! There they are now!"

As Jack spoke he raised his gun and blazed away. This shot was followed by one from Spouter.

The reports were followed almost immediately by a snarl and a whining cry, and they heard some animal thrashing around wildly in the bushes behind the spring, sending the loose snow flying in all directions.

"We hit it, whatever it is," announced Jack.

"What do you suppose it can be?" questioned Spouter quickly. "It wasn't a deer, was it?"

"I don't think so, Spouter. It was too low down for that. Maybe it was a fox, although it didn't sound like it."

"Perhaps there are brook mink around this spring."

"Maybe."

"Are you going back there to find out?" went on Spouter, for the sounds in the brushwood had now ceased.

"Sure, I'm going back there! You don't suppose I'm going to let any game get away from us!"

"Be careful, Jack. That animal may be playing possum, you know, and may spring out at you."

"Don't worry; I'll be on my guard," answered Jack.

Arthur M. Winfield

He had slipped another charge into his gun, and Spouter quickly did likewise. Then, with their weapons ready for use and with the flashlight held so that it cast its rays ahead, they cautiously moved around to one side of the frozen spring and made their way in the direction of the bushes and rocks in the rear.

"Hello there! what are you shooting at?" The cry came from where the pair had left the boxsled. It was Gif who was calling.

"We don't know yet," answered Jack.

"We saw a pair of eyes, and we shot at them," added Spouter.

"Gee! what do you know about that?" exclaimed Fred. "Hunting before we even reach the Lodge!"

"Let's go ahead and see what they struck," came from Randy.

"That's the talk!" added his twin.

Gif was willing, and in a moment more the four lads had scrambled down from the boxsled and were making their way along the road leading to the spring. By this time Jack and Spouter had advanced through the brushwood and over the rocks close to the spot where they had last seen the gleaming eyes. As they went on Jack imagined once or twice he saw something moving through the snow, but of this he was not certain.

"Here is where we hit it, whatever it was," declared Spouter, when they reached the point directly behind the spring. "See how the snow is dug up?"

"Yes, and here are some drops of blood," said Jack, as he turned the flashlight on the snow. "But whatever it was, it got away," he added disappointedly.

"What have you got?" sang out Gif, for he and the others had come up on the opposite side of the spring.

"We haven't got anything," answered Spouter dolefully. "We hit something, but it got away from us."

"It wasn't a moose, was it?" queried Randy with great interest.

"No, I think it was a three-horned elephant," replied Jack, who was not then in the best of humor. He hated to have the first thing he shot at get away from him.

"Well, this seems to be the end of this road," remarked Gif, looking around.

"Yes, it only led down to this frozen-up spring," answered Spouter.

"I move we go on," said Fred. "I'm cold, and I'm sleepy too."

"I think we're all that way," answered Gif. "Come on, you fellows. No use of remaining around here. If that animal got away it probably moved off quite a distance."

"That would depend on how badly it was wounded," answered Jack. "Just wait a minute, and I'll see if I can't find its trail."

Aided by the flashlight, he looked around carefully, and presently made out some tracks in the snow leading in the direction of a nearby thicket. He moved to this, coming presently to several low-hanging trees.

"See anything?" questioned Fred impatiently.

"Not yet. But the trail is here as plain as can be."

"Maybe those are only rabbit tracks," remarked Randy.

"Or tracks of the animals that came down to the spring for a drink," put in Gif.

Jack did not answer. He was flashing the light around carefully, inspecting all the trees and bushes in that vicinity. Suddenly the light was flashed upward, and as the rays ran along one of the branches of the tree directly in front of the youth there came a sudden snarl of rage and protest.

"It's a wildcat!" ejaculated Spouter, whose eyes had also been following the rays of light. "A wildcat!"

"Yes, and it's the animal we wounded," answered Jack. "See how it is holding up one of its front paws."

"Be careful!" sang out Gif, in alarm. "A wounded wildcat is no beast to play with."

Scarcely had he uttered the words when the wildcat gave another snarl of rage. Then the tail of the beast began to quiver, and suddenly, with a cry, it leaped down from the tree, striking the ground directly in front of the surprised boys.

CHAPTER XIII

THE MEETING ON THE ROAD

That the wildcat was in a savage mood and prepared to fight to a finish, there could be no doubt. Evidently the wounded paw had made the beast more savage than usual, and hardly had it struck the ground than it tried to make a leap forward at Jack.

"Look out, Jack!"

"He means to claw you to death!"

Bang! went Spouter's gun, but he did not dare to take too close an aim for fear of hitting Jack, and as a consequence the charge of shot merely damaged the wildcat's tail.

It must not be thought that the oldest Rover was slow in moving. Had this been true, the wildcat would undoubtedly have fastened its claws and its teeth into the youth and done serious damage. As the animal came forward, the young captain leaped to one side and the wildcat landed in the snow, facing the others who had come up.

"Shoot him! Shoot him!" came from Fred excitedly.

Arthur M. Winfield

"Plug him quick!" added Andy.

None of those who had followed Jack and Spouter were armed, so the fight rested entirely upon the shoulders of that pair. Circling around so as to avoid the others, Jack pulled the trigger and fired. The wildcat began flipping and flopping on the snow, badly wounded. Then Spouter discharged his firearm once more, and after this the creature lay quiet where it dropped.

"Is—is he dead?" questioned Fred, who was the first to speak. The youngest Rover was very much excited, and with good cause.

"Wait! Don't go forward!" ordered Jack, as he stepped back a few paces. "He may be playing possum. Anyway, we had better load our guns first," he added to Spouter.

This advice to load immediately after discharging a weapon was one which had been well drilled into the cadets, and so now the pair lost no time in putting new charges into their weapons. Then they approached with caution, and Jack turned the wildcat over with the barrel of the gun, keeping his hand meanwhile on the trigger ready for action.

But the beast was quite dead, the charges from the two guns having gone completely through its body.

"What are you going to do with the carcass?" questioned Randy, after all had made an inspection.

"Might as well leave it here," declared Fred. "It isn't good for anything. Even the skin is all torn from the shot."

"No, we might as well take it along. We can hang it on the back of the boxsled," said Gif. "Perhaps we can use the meat to trap some other wild animals."

A strap which one of the boys happened to carry was fastened around the neck of the wildcat, and then they carried it from the spring to where they had left the boxsled. The excitement for the time being had caused all of the cadets to forget how late it was and how cold and windy it was growing. But now, when they were once more ready to drive off, several of them began to shiver.

"It's going to be mighty cold before morning," announced Randy.

"Yes, and I wish we were at that bungalow in front of a good log fire," added Andy.

"Now that we've discovered that wasn't the road, which way do you propose to go, Gif?" questioned Jack.

"We won't count that as a road, and we'll take the other one on the right," was the reply. "I don't know of anything else to do," Gif added, somewhat helplessly.

None of the others could give advice, for the reason that this territory was entirely new to them. Even Spouter, who had visited the woods a number of times, had never been in that vicinity.

Onward they went once more, up a gentle hill and then down the slope on the other side. At the foot of the hill the road became rougher and rougher, and presently the horses had all they could do to make any progress.

"Gif, this can't be the right road," declared Jack at last. "If it was as rough as this, Jed Wallop would have told us about it. He said we wouldn't have any trouble at all in reaching

Cedar Lodge."

"Yes, and besides, we must have come at least five or six miles," added Spouter.

"I'll bet we've come all of eight miles," broke in Fred.

"That's just what I think," declared Randy. "I'll bet an elephant against a mouse we're on the wrong road."

"Well, I won't dispute that, Randy," answered the young driver of the boxsled. "But you'll all bear witness to it that I followed directions and kept to the right."

The road now ran along the side of a hill. Here the heavy fall of snow had slid down over the rocks and the going was anything but safe. The faithful old horses had all they could do to keep their footing.

"We'll upset the first thing you know!" exclaimed Fred, and he had scarcely spoken when the runner on the up side of the road struck a series of rocks, and the next minute all of the boys, including Gif, went tumbling from the boxsled, and some of their provisions followed.

"Whoa there! Whoa there, Mary and John!" called Gif to the team. But this command was not needed, for the tired old horses were only too glad to stop, and had come to a halt the moment the youths tumbled off.

All had landed in the snow, which at this point was rather deep; so none of them was seriously hurt, although somebody stepped on one of Randy's hands and Spouter got a scratch on his ear from some nearby bushes.

"Well, here's a mess!" exclaimed Fred, as he picked himself

up. "Now we are in a pickle."

"Oh, it might have been worse," declared Jack, as cheerfully as he could, because he could easily see that Gif was in a state of mind bordering on desperation. "Nobody is seriously hurt, I hope?"

All scrambled up, and then looked at the roadway immediately ahead. Here was a somewhat level spot, and to this the sled was driven, and the lads picked up the stuff which had fallen off in the snow and replaced it, this time tying it down with some ropes and straps which were handy.

"I don't believe I'll drive any further on this road," said Gif. "It doesn't seem to lead to anywhere, and I'm quite certain now that it isn't the way to Cedar Lodge."

"What will you do?" asked Andy. "Go back to that other road?"

Everybody was stumped, and for several seconds nobody made any reply.

"Might as well go back," said Spouter.

Fred and Randy walked on ahead, trying to determine where the road led to. But all they could see was the blackness of the forest, and the roadway seemed to grow rougher and more perilous at every step.

It was no easy task to turn the team and the boxsled around without spilling everything again. But it was accomplished at last, and then slowly and painfully they climbed along the hill until they reached the point where there had been another split in the road. Here they came to a halt.

Arthur M. Winfield

"Listen!" cried Randy suddenly.

All did as requested, and from a distance heard the low musical jingle of sleigh bells.

"There's a sleigh!" exclaimed Gif. "And unless I'm mistaken, it's coming this way!"

They listened again, and were overjoyed to note that the sounds were gradually coming nearer. Then they stepped out behind the boxsled, and presently discerned a large two-seated sleigh, drawn by a powerful pair of horses, approaching.

The steeds were making good time, despite the roughness of the road and the depth of the snow.

"Hi there! Hi there!" called out Gif, and then Jack sent the rays of his flashlight toward the on-coming turnout.

There were exclamations of astonishment from those in the sleigh, and for a moment it looked to the boys as if the occupants were bent upon passing them without paying any attention to their call. But then Gif, Spouter, and Fred took a position directly in front of the on-coming horses, and the driver brought them snortingly to a sudden stop.

"What do you fellows want?" demanded a heavy guttural voice from the sleigh.

The words were uttered in a German accent, and by the look of his face the speaker, who sat on the front seat beside the driver, was evidently of Teutonic origin. He glared suspiciously at those in the roadway, and Jack and Gif afterward declared that they saw the gleam of a pistol in the man's hand as it was thrust in the flap of his overcoat.

"We've lost our way," said Gif, coming a few steps closer. "We thought maybe you folks could direct us."

"Huh! I don't know about that," said the man in his thick German accent. "Where do you want to go?"

"We want to go to Cedar Lodge. It's located somewhere up here, about five or six miles from Timminsport."

"Cedar Lodge!" said one of the men who were seated on the rear seat of the sleigh. "Do you mean the hunting lodge that is owned by the Garrisons?"

"Yes."

"Then you are on the wrong road to get to that place," said the man. "You'll have to go back the way we came for about half a mile, and then take the road to the left. It is in from this road, I think, about a quarter of a mile."

"Is it the first road we shall come to from here?" questioned Gif, bound to fix matters so that he could not make another mistake.

"Yes."

"Thank you. That is all we want to know."

"What are you young fellows going to do at that place?" queried the German who was on the front seat.

"We came up here for a season of hunting," answered Jack.

"The place belongs to my father and my uncle," explained Gif. "My name is Gifford Garrison."

"I see. Well, have a good time," said the man on the front seat of the sleigh. But he did not seem to be particularly pleased.

"Have you a hunting lodge around here?" questioned Fred curiously.

"No. We are just taking a little trip to visit some friends up here," answered the man on the back seat who previously had not spoken. "We shall stay only a day or two," he added. Then the man on the front seat spoke to the driver, and away they went once more, and were soon out of sight, taking the road the cadets had just been thinking of pursuing.

"Well, I'm mighty glad we met those men," declared Gif. "Now I know where I am. Thank goodness! we are not so very far out of the way after all."

"Don't crow, Gif, until you are out of the woods—or at least until we are in sight of the Lodge," cried Andy.

"I didn't like the looks of those fellows," declared Jack.

"They were a bunch of Germans, and not very nice Germans at that," said Fred.

"Isn't it queer that we are running into so many Germans?" remarked Spouter. "First that Herman Crouse on the train, and now these chaps."

"Oh, hurry up, fellows! Don't stand here and gas!" ejaculated Randy. "Let's see if we can't find that lost Lodge. I want to get warmed up, and I want to go to bed."

Then the boxsled was turned around once more and the journey to Cedar Lodge was resumed.

CHAPTER XIV

THE FIRST HUNT

The six cadets from Colby Hall found the side road the Germans had mentioned with ease; and after that it was not long before they came to a spot which looked familiar to Gif.

"Thank fortune! we're on the right road at last," cried the young driver of the boxsled. "See those peculiar trees over there?" He pointed to three all growing together. "I know those very well. We ought to come in sight of the Lodge now in a few minutes."

"Well, you can't get there any too quick for me," declared Fred, as he gave a deep yawn.

The way was over a small bridge which spanned the river Gif had mentioned to the Rover boys, and then they passed through a patch of woods and to a clearing about half an acre in extent. In the center of this clearing was located the Lodge.

It was a substantial and artistic log structure, a single story in height, with a broad veranda running the length of the front. Right at either end of the lodge was a huge cedar tree, and more cedars were at the edge of the clearing. Behind the bungalow was a small barn and also a fair-sized woodshed and close by was a small building which Gif explained to them was used in the summer time for a kitchen.

Gif was the first out of the boxsled, and he lost no time in unlocking the front door for the party. Jack brought his flashlight into play, and they lit two lamps after filling them with oil which had been brought along.

"Now we'll get the stuff in from the sled, and then I'll have to put the team away," said Gif.

"Let me do that, Gif," said Jack. "Just show me where they are to go, then you and the others can light the fire."

"Yes, and we'll fix something to eat, too!" declared Randy.

"I'll go out to the stable with Jack," came from Spouter, who was no shirker when it came to doing his share of the work.

It was not a hard task to transfer the baggage and provisions, as well as the guns and team was driven around to the stable, where ammunition, to the Lodge, and, this done, the sled was run in under a shed. Then Jack and Spouter proceeded to make Mary and John at home for the night.

In the meantime all of the others had gone to the woodshed and returned to the Lodge with sticks of various sizes for the fire. The building of this was left to Gif, as it was felt that he was, in a certain sense, the host. Yet all were ready to help, and soon they had a big blaze roaring up the wide chimney and gradually filling the bungalow with its warmth.

The arrangement of the Lodge was very simple. The living room occupied the center, with a sort of winter kitchen and entryway behind it. To each side of the living room were located two bedrooms, one in the front and the other in the rear. Above the living room was a loft which could be reached by a rustic pair of stairs, a loft which could be used only for a storeroom, since it was less than five feet high in the center, sloping to the eaves, front and back. The big chimney was in the rear of the living room, and behind it, in the kitchen, was a stove for cooking.

"Say, this is just all right," declared Fred, after he had warmed up a bit and taken a look around. "We ought to be as snug as bugs in a rug here."

"We'll have to arrange about sleeping quarters," remarked Gif. "Two of the rooms have a double bed each, and the other rooms have two single beds each." The doors to the various rooms had been left open so that the heat from the fire might draw through the entire Lodge.

It was great sport for the boys to divest themselves of their heavy overcoats and caps and then get to work preparing the Lodge for occupancy. All of the bedclothes had to be shaken out and warmed, and they also had to get out some linen which had been packed away. Gif, assisted by Andy and Randy, did this, and meanwhile Jack, Spouter, and Fred brought out the dishes and other things and set the table and also began to boil water for some hot chocolate, which they had decided to have, along with some smoked beef and cheese sandwiches and some doughnuts that had been brought along.

Soon the boys were seated around the big square table the living room contained enjoying themselves to their hearts' content. The steaming chocolate and the things to eat put them in the best possible humor, and their troubles with Bill Glutts and Gabe Werner, and also with the wildcat and on the road, were, for the time being, forgotten. Outside the

Arthur M. Winfield

wind was rising, making a mournful sound as it swept through the cedars and the other trees in that vicinity. But inside the fire crackled merrily and the heat of the fitful flames as they roared up the chimney filled the lads with satisfaction.

"We sure had a tough time getting here," declared Randy, "but it was worth it."

"Isn't this just peachy!" cried his twin, as, with a final doughnut in hand, he sank deep in a rocking chair at one side of the fireplace. "This suits me right down to the tips of my toes."

"I should think it would suit anybody," declared Spouter. "Why, this whole surroundings has the most artistic setting I ever beheld. Just think of this rustic bungalow nestling away in the midst of this gigantic forest, and think of this deep-throated fireplace with the flames soaring upward, casting their flickering shadows hither and thither over the bright faces—"

"Of six well fed and sleepy young fellows who ought to be in bed this minute," broke in Jack. "I move we adjourn for the night and let Spouter finish his oration in the morning."

"That's it! Always cutting me short when I have some beautiful sentiments to express," grumbled the would-be orator. "Never mind, I'll get square with you some day."

"Never mind, Spout. Don't take it too hard," broke in Andy. "Remember that even slipping down on a banana peel is a good deal of a skin game."

"To bed it is," announced Gif. "Unless, of course, Andy and Fred want to remain up to wash the dishes."

"Nothing doing," yawned Fred. "I could go to sleep sitting in this chair. I'll wash the dishes to-morrow morning before breakfast."

It was decided that the twins should occupy one of the rooms with a double bed. Gif and Spouter took the other double bed, and Fred and Jack went into one of the rooms containing two single beds.

"We'll keep the fourth room for possible visitors," announced Gif. "You know, Glutts and Werner may call on us," he added quizzically.

"Of course they'll call—when they are invited!" declared Jack. "Not but what it's your house, Gif," he added quickly.

"They'll never come here on my invitation," was the ready response.

Their previous experience in camping out stood the six cadets in good stead, and they knew exactly how to leave their fire so that it would keep burning until morning without doing any damage. Then, one after another, they speedily shoved off to bed and soon all of them were slumbering peacefully after a long and arduous day's traveling.

In the morning Jack was the first to arise and he was speedily followed by Gif and Spouter.

"Might as well let the others sleep for a while," said the oldest Rover boy. "They were pretty well tired out, Fred and Andy especially."

"Sure, let 'em sleep as long as they want to. Our time is our own, and there is no use in hurrying. Just the same, I bet Fred wakes up pretty quick when he smells boiling coffee and pancakes."

Some pancake flour had been brought along, and soon the appetizing odor of the cakes, along with the odor of steaming coffee, filled the Lodge. Then came a call from one of the bedrooms, and, sure enough, it was Fred speaking.

"Hi there! don't you eat all those good things up before I get there," he called out. "Say! this air certainly gives a fellow an appetite."

By the time breakfast was ready all of the boys were dressed. Jack and Spouter had gone outside for more wood, and they reported that it had begun to snow hard.

"All right, let it snow," said Randy. "Now that we are here, what do we care?"

"Well, we don't want to get snowed in," remarked Spouter.

"Oh, I don't think the storm will be as bad as that," returned Gif. "Just the same, I'm glad we didn't get caught last night in a downfall. We might have had worse luck than ever in getting here."

By the time breakfast was finished it was snowing heavily. There was a fairly strong wind blowing, and this sent the fine particles flying in all directions. When they went out to feed the horses they found the snow already an inch or more in depth.

"I think this is going to add quite a little to what is already on the ground," said Jack. "If it keeps on for any length of time it will make hunting rather difficult."

"Why can't we go out and do some hunting before the storm

gets too bad?" questioned Fred. Now that he had reached the Lodge he was exceedingly anxious to try his skill with a gun.

"When I was here before there was quite a rabbit run on the other side of the cedars behind this bungalow," declared Gif. "It isn't a long way off. We could easily go that distance even through the snow."

"There wouldn't be any chance of our losing our way?" queried Spouter.

"Oh, no. It's not far enough off for that."

"Then let's go before the storm gets any worse," cried Andy.

"Yes, but how about the dishes to be washed?" asked Gif.

"Oh, Gif, can't we do them just as soon as we get back?" questioned Fred.

"Last night's dishes are still standing in the kitchen," declared Jack, looking somewhat sternly at his cousins.

"We'll get at them the minute we get back from our hunt for rabbits!" exclaimed Fred. "Won't we, Andy?"

"That's a contract," declared the fun-loving Rover.

"All right then, see that you keep your word," answered Jack. "Remember, Gif, no more grub for anybody until the dishes are washed."

"It's too bad we didn't bring some wooden dishes with us," remarked Randy. "Then, after we had used them, we could put 'em in the fire."

"Lazybones!" called out Spouter. "You are as bad as the tramp who said he didn't care to eat prunes because it was such a job to spit out the pits;" and at this there was a general smile.

A little later the boys were ready for their first hunt. They had discarded their overcoats for a number of hunting jackets of which the bungalow boasted, and had also donned leggings and caps. Each looked to see that his weapon was in first-class order and that he had a sufficient supply of ammunition.

"We'll take only the shotguns along," said Gif. "You won't find any big game in this immediate vicinity."

Fixing the fire so that it would keep until they returned, they locked up and then started away. The snow was still coming down steadily, and they were glad when they reached the shelter of the woods.

"You don't suppose Jed Wallop will come here during our absence?" questioned Jack.

"If he does he'll know what to do," answered Gif. "He knows where the key to the bungalow is, and I left a note for him in the stable, stating that if he wanted to take the team away he could do so. He usually keeps the horses up at his place, which is about half a mile from here."

Forward they trudged along a narrow trail leading through the woods. Gif was at the front, with Spouter and Jack close behind and the others following. Feeling that the rabbits might be on the alert, they relapsed into silence, making practically no noise as they advanced.

They had covered a distance of several hundred feet when

Jack, happening to glance overhead, saw something that interested him very much. A flock of wild ducks was circling about, and he pointed them out to Gif.

"I have often seen 'em around here," whispered Gif. "But you'd have to go a long distance to get 'em unless you could shoot 'em on the wing. They never settle down in the vicinity of the bungalow."

"Some day I'm going to take a crack at them," said Jack. "That is, if they fly low enough."

Presently Gif slowed his pace and motioned for the others to do likewise. They had come out to where there was a small clearing. Here all gazed around sharply, trying to find some trace of the rabbit run Gif had mentioned.

"I see one!" exclaimed Spouter presently. "See him? Over yonder," and he pointed with his hand.

"Yes! And there is another!" answered Jack.

"I see four or five of them," put in Gif.

"Oh, say! there is our chance," ejaculated Fred excitedly. "Let's get busy at once," and he made as if to raise his shotgun.

"Don't fire yet," cautioned Jack. "We're not close enough."

"Come on! I'll show you a place where we'll have a good chance to get at those rabbits," said Gif. "Come, follow me."

Arthur M. Winfield

CHAPTER XV

A CRY FOR HELP

Making as little noise as possible, the other lads followed Gif back into the woods and then along a snow-laden trail skirting the clearing.

Less than two minutes' walk brought the young hunters to a spot where were located a series of rough rocks, and here Gif motioned for his companions to halt.

"I think you will find the rabbits in the hollow just on the other side of these rocks," he whispered. "Now get you guns ready before you show yourselves."

Slowly and cautiously they mounted the rocks and then lay down in the snow on top. They peered into the hollow below, and presently made out the forms of at least a dozen rabbits running to and fro, evidently trying to find something among the trees and bushes opposite that would be fit to eat.

"We might as well fire all at the same time," said Jack. "Because after the first shot those bunnies will do their best to get to cover."

It was quickly decided that some of the hunters should shoot at the rabbits directly ahead, while others were to shoot at those to the right or to the left.

It must be admitted that Fred and Andy were trembling with excitement, and Randy was also agitated. The others were quite calm, or else they did not allow their real feelings to show. It was decided that Jack should give the order to fire.

"All right," said the oldest Rover boy. "Now take aim, and when I say three, shoot."

There were several seconds of silence during which all of the young hunters got in readiness to shoot. Then, while they were still aiming their weapons, one of the rabbits suddenly stopped running around and sat upright, directly facing them, with his long ears pointed skyward.

"Quick!" exclaimed Jack excitedly. "They see us! One—two—three! Fire!"

The six shotguns spoke almost as one piece, and as the reports echoed across the clearing and through the woods, several of the rabbits were seen to leap into the air and then fall back lifeless. Several others were seriously wounded, and these were speedily put out of their misery by a second shot from Gif and Spouter.

"Hurrah! Seven rabbits!" exclaimed Fred, running forward. "That's what I call a pretty good start."

"Come on, let us go after the others! Leave these where they are," cried Jack, and plunged into the wood where he had seen several of the rabbits seeking refuge. He managed to bring down one of them, and Randy brought down another. The others got away.

Arthur M. Winfield

"Nine rabbits is by no means a bad haul," was Gif's comment, after the boys had brought the dead game together.

"Enough for a splendid potpie, and then some," came from Spouter.

"Do you suppose we can get any more?" exclaimed Andy. He was quite certain he had brought down one of the bunnies.

"We can try, Andy," answered Gif. "It isn't late yet, and the snow isn't so deep but what it might be deeper."

Having divided the rabbits between them, so that each lad might carry some of the game, they moved forward, across the little clearing, and then through the woods for the best part of a quarter of a mile. During that time they saw several squirrels, but were unable to get a shot at the frisky animals.

"A squirrel is as quick as they make 'em," declared Gif. "You've got to act like lightning to catch 'em."

By this time it was snowing so heavily that all concluded it would be a wise move to return to Cedar Lodge. The wind was rising, shaking the tops of the trees violently and causing a strange moaning sound through the thickets which was anything but pleasant.

"I'd hate to be caught out here all alone and in the darkness," remarked Randy to Fred, as they trudged along.

"Would give a fellow the creeps, wouldn't it?" was the reply.

As they continued on their way they kept their eyes wide open for the possible appearance of more game. But no animals showed themselves, nor did they see any birds circling through the snow, which seemed every moment to be coming down thicker than ever.

"If this snow continues and the wind keeps on rising, we'll have a regular blizzard before morning," announced Gif.

"Don't say a word about the wind," panted Andy, who had dropped a few paces behind, "My nose and my ears are almost frozen."

"Well, thank goodness, Andy, we're not very far from the Lodge. You'll soon be able to warm up."

They were still deep in the woods when from a distance they heard a peculiar whistle twice repeated.

"That's Jed Wallop's whistle," announced Gif. "He must have just come in."

He whistled in return, and presently they came out at a point where the cedars fringed the clearing in the midst of which was located the bungalow. They saw Jed Wallop standing outside the little stable and waved their hands to him, and he waved in return.

"Thought you might have gone out huntin'," announced Wallop, when they came up. "Had some luck, too, I see."

"Nine rabbits," said Fred, a bit proudly.

"Good enough! I guess that means some good, old-fashioned rabbit stew to-night," and Jed Wallop grinned.

He had not seen Gif's note, and so the lads explained the situation, to which the man listened with much concern.

"Well, by gum! what do you know about that?" he ejaculated. "I certain did mix it when I give you them directions. I might o' told you about turnin' to the left when it come to the road past this lodge. You see, I got all twisted up in my mind as soon as I heard about my cousin, Tim Doolittle, bein' hurt."

"That's just the way I figured it, Jed," answered Gif. "However, as we got here at last it doesn't matter."

"Goin' to have a pretty good fall o' snow, boys;" and Jed Wallop looked anxiously at the sky.

"Do you think we shall be snowed in?" questioned Randy.

"Might be—if the storm keeps up long enough. But you got plenty o' provisions, ain't you?"

"Oh, we've got enough to last us for a week or ten days," answered Gif.

"Then I guess you'll be all right. But say! maybe you fellers would like me to stay here with you?" continued Jed Wallop. "Not but wot you're big enough to take care of yourselves."

"We'll get along all right, Jed. Don't worry," answered Gif.

"Then I'll be a-takin' the team and gettin' over to my own place," announced the man. "And I won't lose no time, nuther. I don't want to git stuck on the road with Mary and John. They are a purty good team, but they are apt to loose heart if the wind gits to blowin' too strong agin 'em."

"How is your cousin getting along?" questioned Jack kindly.

"Oh, he's a-doin' tolerable. I took him over to our Uncle

Joe's, you know, and the women folks over there will give him the best o' care."

The boys assisted Jed Wallop to hook up the team to the boxsled, and in a few minutes more the man was off with a crack of his whip, which sent the team away at a fairly respectable pace.

"Now, have a good time!" he called back to the boys. "And don't shoot all the game in the State."

"When will you be back?" sang out Spouter.

"In a few days. If you want me before that time give the signal;" for it had been arranged that when the boys wanted Jed Wallop to come over from where he lived they were to shoot a gun two times twice in succession.

"He won't have any sweet job of it getting to his place," announced Fred.

"Fortunately, it isn't a great distance off," answered Gif. "If he had several miles to go, I doubt if he would be able to make it."

Shutting up the stable and loading their arms with firewood from the shed, the six cadets made their way into the Lodge. When they opened the door the wind rushed in, causing the sparks and the ashes from the smouldering fire to fly in all directions.

"Shut that door!" Gif cried quickly. "My, how that wind is rising!"

"Maybe it'll blow the bungalow over," remarked Randy.

Arthur M. Winfield

"Oh, I don't believe it will get as bad as all that, Randy," said Jack. "This looks as if it was a pretty substantial building."

"You're right," came from Gif. "Those logs are good and heavy, and they were put together by some of the best workmen around here. This house won't go down unless the woods go down with it. But I am mighty glad we are under shelter where we can take it comfortable."

"Do you know what I think?" said Fred. "I think we ought to bring in more of that firewood. There is no telling if we'll be able to get any of it by morning if this snow keeps coming down."

"A good idea, Fred," said Jack. "Let us go out at once and pile all the wood we can in the entryway beside the kitchen."

Leaving Gif to stir up the fire so that the Lodge might get warm once more, the others hurried out to the woodshed. They made four trips from that place to the entryway beside the kitchen, each time bringing in all the logs they could carry.

"There! that wood ought to last us for two or three days," declared Jack, when the task was done.

"Now I know what I'm going to do," said Fred, as they re-entered the main building.

"What's that?" queried Spouter.

"I'm going to get at those dishes."

"So are we!" declared Andy and Randy in a breath.

Water was heated, and it did not take long to dispose of the dirty dishes. While the three boys were doing this, the others cleaned up the living room of the bungalow, and also straightened out their beds. From time to time all gazed out of the small-paned windows, to see that the snow was coming down as thickly as ever.

"We're in for it, and no mistake," said Gif finally. "I don't think we'll be able to do much hunting for a day or two."

"Well, that will give us a good chance to rest," declared Jack. "I don't know but what I would just as lief take a nap after lunch. That tramp in the wind after the rabbits made me sleepy."

All were rather tired, and as a consequence the lunch was an informal affair, the boys warming up and opening a large can of pork and beans and making themselves a large pot of steaming chocolate.

"We'll have dinner to-night," said Gif, and to this the others agreed.

Then they cleared the dishes away and took it easy, some resting in front of the fire and others on the beds in the rooms.

"If it gets much colder we'll have to pull some of those beds out into the living room and close the doors to the bedrooms," announced Gif. "I remember we did that one time when I was up here."

By five o'clock the boys felt rested, and then began preparations for a regular dinner. Several of the rabbits were cleaned and cooked, and they also boiled some potatoes and onions. Then Gif and Jack prepared a pan of biscuits and a pot of tea.

Arthur M. Winfield

"Some day I'm going to take a few hours off and make some pies and cakes," announced Randy. He had always had a great liking for desserts.

"Yes, and don't forget we're going to make some candy, too," added his twin.

In the evening the boys read some magazines they had brought along, and Jack and Spouter played checkers. Before retiring, they looked out of the windows, to find that it was snowing and blowing just as furiously as ever.

"It's going to be a wild night, believe me," announced Spouter. "I don't believe there will be many people traveling around in this vicinity."

They retired as they had done the night before, and soon, despite the whistling of the wind, all of the lads were sound asleep.

Suddenly Jack awakened with a start. How long he had been asleep he did not know. He sat up quickly, for he realized that some sound from without had awakened him.

"Help! Help!" came from outside the bungalow. "Help! Let us in! We're freezing to death!"

CHAPTER XVI

UNDESIRABLE VISITORS

"Wake up, Fred! There is somebody at the door trying to get in!" called out Jack, as the cry from outside was repeated.

"What's that? What's the matter?" came sleepily from the other Rover boy.

From outside came a feeble kicking and pounding on the main door to the Lodge. Two boys were calling piteously for assistance.

"Get up, everybody!" sang out Jack, as he jumped up and stuck his feet into a pair of slippers which were handy.

His call and the noise from outside aroused Gif and Spouter, as well as Fred, and soon the four cadets were hurrying into the living room. They wore nothing but their pajamas, and slippers, but now each slipped hastily into his overcoat.

"Who is it?" demanded Gif, for he had no desire to have the Lodge overrun by a crowd of noisy and possibly half-drunken lumberjacks.

"It's us—Bill Glutts and Gabe Werner," was the faint reply.

"Please leave us in before we are frozen to death."

"Werner and Glutts!" ejaculated Fred. And now the continued noise brought Andy and Randy on the scene.

"What can they be doing out here this time of night?" demanded Fred.

"Say, let us in, won't you?" came pleadingly in Gabe Werner's voice. "You don't want to let us freeze to death, do you?"

"What brought you here this time of night?" demanded Jack.

"We're on our way to Tony Duval's place," answered Gabe Werner. "But the storm is so fierce we couldn't get any further. Our horse is completely winded."

"You are sure you are alone?" demanded Gif.

"Yes, yes! Please let us in. My nose and ears are frozen."

"And I don't know whether I've got any feet left or not," broke in Bill Glutts piteously.

The main door to the bungalow had not only been locked, but also barred. Now the door was unfastened, and Gif, with the others beside him, allowed the portal to swing open a few inches.

A terrible scene met their eyes. The snow was piled up against the door to the depth of two feet or more, and the wind was swirling the white particles in all directions, so that the snow came into the living room in a perfect cloud. In this mass of white stood Bill Glutts and Gabe Werner, their heavy clothing covered with a ghost-like mantle. Behind them was a one-seated sleigh drawn by a horse that looked ready to drop from exhaustion.

"Come in," said Gif briefly.

No such invitation was needed, for as soon as the door was opened wide enough Bill Glutts staggered into the living room, followed by his crony. A swirl of snow followed them, and continued until Gif and Jack managed to close the door once more.

"Gee! I'm all in," gasped Glutts, as he sank down on a chair close to the smouldering fire.

"I thought we'd drop before we got you fellows up," added Werner. "You sure are some sleepers," he grumbled, as he too sank down on a seat.

Ordinarily the Rovers and their chums would have treated these two bullies with scant courtesy. But now Glutts and Werner appeared to be suffering so much from the cold that they had not the heart to find fault with their enemies.

"I'll stir up that fire a little," said Gif, and did so while Andy and Randy went out into the entryway, to bring in some additional sticks of wood.

"We can't leave that horse out there," remarked Jack. "He'll be frozen to death."

"Well, I'm not going out to take care of him," declared Gabe Werner quickly. "I wouldn't go out in that storm again for a thousand dollars."

"Neither would I," growled Glutts. "The nag can look after himself."

"That's a shameful way to treat any animal, Glutts," declared Gif. "But as you fellows seem to be so exhausted, we'll look after him," he continued.

"If you go out, Gif, I'll go with you," said Jack quickly. "But we had better slip some of our clothing right over our pajamas. I'll bet it's as cold as Greenland's icy mountains around that stable."

While the newcomers continued to make themselves comfortable before the fire, and Spouter and Fred prepared a pot of hot tea for them to drink, Gif and Jack hurried into their clothing and then went outside.

The blast that struck them as they hurried toward the exhausted horse was terrific, and for the moment they thought they would have to turn back and abandon the animal. But then they took another grip on themselves, and finally managed to turn the horse in the direction of the stable.

They saw that the sleigh was filled with provisions and other things, and so managed to haul it under the shed where it would be partly protected. Then they placed the horse in the stable, gave him a drink, and likewise left some hay for him to chew on.

"We may not be able to get here in the morning," said Gif; "so we'll leave him some supper and some breakfast at the same time."

"I don't much like the idea of Glutts and Werner loading down on us in this fashion," remarked Jack, as the pair prepared to go back to the Lodge.

"Like it!" exclaimed his chum. "I should say not! But what

are we going to do about it, Jack?"

"Oh, we'll have to make the best of it."

"If this storm keeps up we may have those fellows on our hands for some days."

"Well, if they stay here that long they can pay their own way," declared Jack. "They have some provisions in that sleigh, and there is no reason why we should feed them for nothing. If we divide up our stuff they can divide up theirs."

"It wouldn't be any more than fair."

"Where is this Tony Duval's place they mentioned?" continued the oldest Rover boy.

"It's about two miles from here, off to the eastward—in fact, the road on which this Lodge is located ends at Duval's place. He is a French-Canadian, and he hasn't a very good reputation in these parts. Some of the old hunters used to think Tony was a good deal of a thief—that he would go around in the night or early morning and empty their traps. He came from down east."

"What do you suppose Werner and Glutts are going to do there?"

"Of late years Duval has made a specialty of hiring out his place to hunters. There are two or three shacks on his land, and he lets the various crowds have those buildings, and then, if the hunters want it, he cooks for them, for he is said to be quite a handy man with a coffeepot and a frying pan. More than likely, from what you heard at the moving picture theater, Gabe Werner has a chance to use one of those shacks and has got Glutts to go with him."

"I wonder why Codfish isn't with them—he was at that restaurant in Timminsport."

"I'm sure I don't know, except that Codfish may have got cold feet when it came to traveling up this way in such a snowstorm. You know there is nothing brave about that little sneak." And in this surmise Gif was correct. Stowell had found a boarding place in the town and had said he would remain there until the storm cleared away and the others returned to get him.

In the meantime Glutts and Werner were seated at the living-room table drinking the hot tea which had been prepared and eating some doughnuts which Fred and Andy had offered. The bullies had become thawed out, and their usual aggressiveness was beginning to assert itself.

"Of course we could have kept on until we got up to Tony's place; but what was the use on such a wild night as this when we knew this place was handy?" remarked Werner.

"I'm afraid you're going to be snowed in with us," said Spouter.

"Huh! I don't know as that will be very pleasant," grumbled Glutts. "Have you fellows got enough for all hands to eat?" he demanded eagerly.

"We've got some provisions," answered Fred cautiously. "We shot nine rabbits to-day," he added proudly.

"Nine rabbits!" exclaimed Werner. "How did you do it?"

"They must have driven the poor rabbits together in a bunch and then slaughtered them," was Glutts' comment.

"We did not!" cried Fred.

"I'm sure we'll get all the rabbits we want when we reach Tony Duval's place," continued Werner boastfully. "I believe hunting up there is much better than it is around here."

"And they tell me Tony is one of the best guides in these parts," added Glutts. "We expect to get a deer or two and a whole lot of other game."

"Say, have you fellows got a place where we can sleep?" questioned the other bully, looking around the living room.

"There is a bedroom here that is not being used," answered Spouter. "But you'll have to ask Gif about that. This bungalow, you know, belongs to Mr. Garrison and his brother."

When Gif and Jack returned the situation was explained to them, and Gif said that for the balance of the night the two newcomers could occupy the bedroom which was not in use.

"And then we'll see what can be done to-morrow morning," he added.

"Of course we'll pay for our accommodations," said Werner, in his most lordly manner.

"We don't want any pay, Werner," declared Gif. "But if you have to stay here very long you'll have to divide your stores with us. It is quite a task to get new stuff all the way from Timminsport; so if you've got anything in the sleigh outside it won't be any more than fair for you to divide with us."

"What did you do with the sleigh and the stuff?"

"We placed it under the shed next to the stable and covered your stuff with a horse blanket. The snow is sifting in there some, but I don't think anything will get hurt; unless, of course, you've got some stuff that might freeze."

"Let it freeze," grumbled Glutts. "I'm not going out again, now I'm comfortable here."

As there was no love lost between the newcomers and our friends, the conversation languished after this. Gif showed Glutts and Werner where they might sleep in the bedroom which had not been occupied, and gave them the necessary bedding and some extra blankets. Then the pair shoved off without even saying good-night and closed the door behind them.

"Real loving and thankful—I don't think," whispered Randy.

"I don't see why those fellows were wished on us," growled his twin. "I'd just as lief have a skunk in the place as to have either of that pair."

"Well, we couldn't leave them out in the storm to perish," answered Jack, in a low tone; "so we'll have to make the best of it."

"Just the same," whispered Fred, "I'm going to keep my eyes and ears wide open while they are here."

CHAPTER XVII

NEW YEAR'S DAY IN CAMP

When Randy and Andy retired it was a long while before the merry twins could get to sleep again.

"We ought to play some good joke on them," was the way Andy expressed it. "Something they would remember."

"I'd do it in a minute, Andy, if it wasn't that they are so worn out," responded his twin. "But I don't think Jack and Fred would like it at all if we disturbed 'em. And, besides, you must remember that while we are here we're Gif's guests."

Gif and Jack were the first to get up in the morning, and they had the fire revived and breakfast underway before any of the others showed themselves.

"Where are Glutts and Werner?" questioned Spouter, when he appeared.

"They haven't showed themselves yet, Spouter," answered Jack. "Might as well let them sleep as long as they want to. They can't leave here in such a storm as this."

The snow was still coming down and the wind was blowing

Arthur M. Winfield

almost as fiercely as it had during the early part of the night. Gazing through the windows, the cadets saw that all of the cedars were bent down with the weight of the fine white crystals. The snow had swept up along one side of the little barn until there was an unbroken line reaching up to the very top.

"Well, I never!" ejaculated Jack, turning around suddenly to his chums. "Happy New Year, everybody!"

"Happy New Year!" came from the others, including Fred and the twins, who had just got up.

"Gosh! I forgot all about it's being New Year's," exclaimed Fred.

"This looks like a real New Year's Day, and no mistake," remarked Randy. "Look outside! Isn't it just like a picture on a New Year's card?"

"It is assuredly a spectacle to fill one with awe and reverence," came from Spouter. "Just gaze upon that magnificent stretch of snowy mantle and those tall cedars bending low before the wintry blasts! Can you imagine what this must be in the solemn depth of the mighty forest, where not a footfall is heard nor a—"

"Jack rabbit can get as much as a turnip to eat?" finished Randy gayly. "Spouter, if you are going to orate, why don't you stand on the table when you turn on the spigot?"

"Let us have a regular New Year's dinner!" cried Gif, "and then Spouter can do the speech-making—"

"While we do the eating," finished Randy. "Say, Spout, how about it?"

"Nothing doing," was the prompt reply. "I want my share of the eats every time."

"We'll make a regular rabbit potpie to take the place of turkey," announced Gif.

"And for dessert, how about that canned plum pudding we brought along?" queried Fred.

"Great thought, Fred!" answered Randy. "And we can have some of those nuts, too. And to-night we'll try our hand at some candy making."

"One thing you fellows are forgetting," remarked Gif. "And that is that we have Werner and Glutts with us. They'll certainly want their share of the good things."

"What! Plum pudding and all?" questioned Fred, with a gloomy look settling over his face.

"We can't deny them anything that we have ourselves, Fred," replied Jack.

"I don't think Glutts or Werner deserve it!" exclaimed Randy. "I think as soon as this storm clears away they ought to be sent about their business. It isn't so very far to that Tony Duval's place, and with their horse and sleigh they ought to be able to make it somehow."

Randy had scarcely finished speaking when the door to the bedroom the two bullies occupied was flung open and Werner strode into the living room.

"Fine way you have of talking about us, Rover!" he said, with a sour look on his face. "We didn't come here because we wanted to. We came because it was necessary."

"And we said we would pay for whatever we had to eat or drink," added Glutts, who had followed his crony.

"I told you before that you wouldn't have to pay a cent," broke in Gif. "Just the same, Glutts, we might as well come to an understanding. You know as well as I do that there is no love lost between you fellows and our crowd. You are welcome to stay here and have your dinner, and if you think you can't get out to-day you can stay here for supper and sleep here again to-night. By that time I think the storm will have cleared away, and you will be able to get over to Tony's place without trouble."

"You can take it from me, we won't stay here an hour longer than we have to," declared Werner. And then he turned back into the bedroom to finish his dressing, closing the door behind him.

The presence of the two bullies put a good deal of a damper on our friends, and as a consequence the breakfast was rather a silent one. Then Gif suggested that Glutts and Werner go out and look after their horse, and this they agreed to do.

"If you won't take any pay we'll stand for our share of the grub," announced Werner just before he went out. "We've got some goods in the sleigh, as you know. What shall I bring in?"

"Bring in whatever you think is fair," said Gif, after a few whispered words to Jack and Spouter.

The two bullies were gone the best part of an hour, and during that time the Rovers and their chums cleaned several of the rabbits and also got ready some potatoes and turnips for dinner.

"That will give us quite a meal, along with the dried lima beans that I put to soak last night," said Gif. "Of course, we'll have the plum pudding, well steamed, as Fred suggested."

"And we'll make a pan of biscuits, too," added Spouter. "Gee! by the time we get through up here, fellows, we'll be able to get jobs as chefs in some of the first-class New York hotels."

When Glutts and Werner returned they carried two packages which they threw on the living-room table.

"There are some dried apricots and a package of rice," said Werner. "They ought to help out for a New Year's dinner."

"Very well, we'll cook what we need for the meal, Werner," said Gif briefly, "and the rest you can take with you."

Gif and Spouter made a small rice pudding, and also stewed some of the apricots. All told, the New Year's dinner proved to be quite a bountiful affair, and after all of the lads had eaten their fill, it must be confessed that everybody felt in better humor. The plum pudding especially came in for a large share of their attention, as well as did the nuts and the small amount of raisins which followed.

"I think we'll go and take a nap," announced Werner presently. "I didn't get very much sleep last night."

"And I'll do the same," added Glutts.

"What about washing those dishes?" remarked Fred, with a significant look at the two bullies.

"That's right, Glutts and Werner!" cried Jack. "You ought to be willing to do your share of the dish-washing."

"Me wash dishes!" roared Bill Glutts. "I never did anything like that in my life!"

"You washed your own dishes at the encampment," answered Spouter sharply.

"Oh, well, that was different."

"Oh, don't gas," grumbled Werner. "We'll wash our own dishes, anyway," and he went to work without another word, although with very bad grace, and presently Glutts followed him.

Gif and the other boys also took hold, so the dish-washing and the pot cleaning did not take very long.

The majority of the boys felt sleepy, so the rest of the day was spent in taking it easy or in reading. Then, toward night, they had a light supper, and Fred and the twins started to make some home-made candy.

By this time the storm had cleared away; no more snow was coming down and the wind had also ceased. Overhead the stars glittered like so many diamonds.

"It will be a great day to-morrow," announced Gif.

"Perhaps we can get out and get on the track of a deer!" cried Fred.

"Say, Fred, you must think the deer in this vicinity are standing around just waiting to be shot," came from Jack, with a smile.

"I don't care, Jack. I'm going to get a crack at something worth while before I go home," announced the youngest Rover.

Declining to partake of the taffy and the nut candy the twins and Fred had made, Glutts and Werner retired early.

"We'll be going in the morning if the storm will permit it," said Werner to Gif. And then he added curtly: "Much obliged for taking us in."

"Don't mention it, Werner," answered Gif, just as briefly.

"Remember, we'll pay you if you'll tell us how much it is," added Glutts.

"You can't pay me anything, Glutts."

"Just as you say."

Then the door to the bedroom was closed as before, and Gif and his chums were left to themselves.

"Some New Year's Day, believe me," was Fred's whispered comment. "The presence of those fellows is about as cheering as a funeral."

Randy and Andy had their heads close together and were whispering. Presently Randy got up and stretched himself.

"Now that it has stopped snowing I am going to go out and get a little fresh air in my lungs," he remarked.

"And I'm going along," responded his twin quickly.

"So am I," broke in Fred.

"And that means we can wash the dishes," said Jack. "All right, there are only a handful anyway. Go ahead, only don't walk too far and get lost."

The three lads were soon outside, ploughing around through the deep snow. Then Randy caught Fred by the arm.

"Come on down to the stable," he said. "Andy and I have a little something up our sleeves."

"Just what I thought," chuckled Fred, "I bet you're planning to play some trick on Glutts and Werner."

"Can you blame us?" demanded Andy.

"Certainly not. I'm with you. What do you propose to do?"

"We want to find out first what those fellows are carrying in the way of provisions. Quite something, I imagine."

Reaching the stable, the three Rovers passed around one corner to where was located the shed. Here they found the sleigh and its contents just as it had been left by Glutts and Werner when they had procured the rice and the apricots. Randy carried a flashlight, and this was turned on so they might see what was stored there.

"A pretty complete lot of stuff," was Randy's comment, after they had looked over the various bundles and packages, each one of which was marked.

"Here is a bag of sugar and another bag of salt," announced Andy. "I think the flavor of each will be vastly improved by mixing them up a bit," and he grinned.

"And here's a bottle of vinegar and two bottles of catsup and maple syrup," came from Randy. "I think a little mixing up here will help matters also."

"Say, don't go too far!" cried Fred in alarm.

"Too far!" exclaimed Randy. "You couldn't go too far with Gabe Werner and Bill Glutts! Just remember what they did to us at Colby Hall and at the encampment. Both of those fellows are nothing but rascals. They didn't deserve to be taken in."

After that Fred joined the twins in "doctoring up the provisions," as Andy expressed it. The three had quite some fun doing this, and all returned to the bungalow grinning broadly.

"There will be something doing when they start to use those stores," chuckled Andy. "My, won't Glutts and Werner be mad!"

"They won't know we did it," returned his twin.

"They won't know it," answered Fred, "but they'll take it for granted, nevertheless. I'll tell you, fellows, I don't know about this," he added dubiously.

"Oh, don't worry," answered Andy gayly. "Gabe Werner and Bill Glutts deserve all that they are getting, and more too."

CHAPTER XVIII

FISHING THROUGH THE ICE

With nothing of importance to do and nobody to awaken them, the Rover boys and their chums slept late the next morning. Gif was the first to get up, and, seeing that the others were still asleep, he made as little noise as possible when he went out into the living-room to stir up the smouldering fire and place upon it a couple of extra logs.

"Hello, Gif! Up already?" came from Spouter, when the other cadet came back to finish his dressing. "What sort of a day is it?"

"Clear as crystal, Spouter. It couldn't be better."

"Then perhaps we'll get a chance to go out hunting."

"Perhaps." Gif looked doubtful for a moment. "I don't know that I care to leave this place until Glutts and Werner have gone."

"I don't blame you, Gif. It would be just like those mean chaps to try to do some damage before they left. They are not the kind to appreciate in the least what we have done for them."

"Hardly—after the way they kicked up about washing a few dishes. It made me sick."

Gif and Spouter began preparations for breakfast, and while they were at this the four Rovers appeared, one after another. The door to the room turned over to Glutts and Werner remained closed.

"Those fellows are certainly putting in some sleep," was Jack's comment.

"Shall I wake 'em up?" questioned Fred quickly.

"No. Let them take their own time," answered Gif. "With such fine weather they ought to have no trouble in getting away, and there is no use of another row before they start."

The lads prepared a generous breakfast of pancakes and some sausage meat that had been brought along from Timminsport, washed down with a copious supply of hot coffee. As they ate they cast sundry glances at the closed bedroom door, but saw no sign of Glutts or Werner.

"Gee! they must be sleeping like rocks," was Andy's comment.

"You'd think the smell of the pancakes and sausage would wake 'em up on such a cold morning as this," added his twin. "My! but it's good!"

"Perhaps they thought they wouldn't bother us about breakfast and take it out in sleep instead," suggested Fred.

"Say, did any of you fellows get up during the night to get something to eat—crackers or cheese, or anything like that?" questioned Gif quickly.

All of the others shook their heads.

"What makes you ask that question, Gif?" remarked Jack.

"Why, I saw a lot of crumbs scattered over the kitchen table and on the floor."

"Maybe Glutts and Werner got up to get something—" began Fred, and then a sudden idea came into his mind and he gave a start. "Gee! what would you say if they were gone?"

"Gone!" echoed the others.

"Maybe they're not in that room at all!" added Jack.

"I'll soon find out!" answered Gif, and, leaving the breakfast table, he went over and tried the bedroom door. It was unlocked, and he opened it and went inside.

"They're gone, all right enough," he called out, and immediately the others followed him into the room. Here they found the beds mussed up and empty. All of the things belonging to Glutts and Werner were gone and the single window of the room was wide open.

"That's a fine way to leave, I must say," grumbled Gif.

"Yes, and to leave this window wide open so the room can get as cold as a barn!" added Spouter, as he pulled down the sash. "Some mean fellows, believe me!"

"Let's see if the horse and sleigh are gone too!" cried Randy.

In a few minutes he and Fred were ready to go out, and they lost no time in hurrying down to the barn and the shed. Sure enough, the horse and sleigh were gone, and the barn door had been left wide open.

"I wonder when they went," remarked Fred.

"Most likely as soon as it was daylight. They probably had this all fixed last night. That's why they went to bed early."

"Well, it doesn't hurt my feelings to have them missing."

"I'd like to know if they took any of our things with them."

The two Rovers returned to the Lodge, and there told of what they had discovered. A search around the Lodge was immediately instituted, the boys looking over their clothing and firearms and then their stores and the regular belongings of the bungalow.

"As far as I can make out, there is only one flannel blanket from the bed missing," said Gif. "I suppose they took that along to keep warm on the ride. They didn't have but one small robe in the sleigh."

"I don't know about these stores," announced Spouter, who had been going over them carefully. "It seems to me we had more canned stuff than this—some green corn and asparagus, and also some canned salmon and sardines."

"I wouldn't put it past 'em to take anything they thought they needed," declared Fred. "They are just that sort, and everybody here knows it."

"All I can say is, 'Good riddance to bad rubbish,'" said Randy.

"And may we fail to see 'em again while we're in this vicinity," added his twin.

"My! but it's a real relief to have them gone," announced Jack. "Now we can do as we please and have the best times ever," and his face showed his pleasure.

Everybody felt glad to think the two bullies were gone, and soon they were chatting gayly. Then, after the breakfast dishes had been put away, all went outside and there indulged in a snowball fight which lasted the best part of the morning.

After such a glorious time in the open, all the cadets ought to have felt in the best of spirits, but it was observed by Jack at dinner time that Fred and the twins looked rather preoccupied. They were whispering together, and presently Randy spoke.

"I and Andy and Fred have been thinking that perhaps it would be best for us to let you other fellows know how matters stand," said he. "Maybe you won't approve of what we did. Just the same, we think Glutts and Werner deserve it." And thereupon he and the others related what had been done the evening before down at the shed. All of the others had to grin at the recital, yet Jack and Gif shook their heads.

"I don't blame you," said the oldest Rover boy. "Just the same, it may lead to more trouble."

"If they find out that you did it, they'll probably come here and try to pay us back," was Gif's comment.

"Let them come," announced Spouter. "I guess we can hold our own against them. I am glad we did something for them to remember us by, especially if they walked off with some of our stuff."

That afternoon the boys went hunting again, but on account

of the heavy fall of snow did not go any great distance. They managed, however, to get two more rabbits, and also two squirrels, and two quail.

"Well, that's something, anyhow," declared Fred, who had laid one of the squirrels low. "A bird and squirrel potpie won't go bad for a change."

"Right-o!" cried Andy.

"Say, Gif, what's the matter with trying our hand at fishing through the ice?" questioned Jack. "The deep snow ought not to interfere with that sport."

"Just as you say. We can go down to the river to-morrow if the crowd is willing."

The day passed without their seeing or hearing any more of Werner and Glutts, nor did anyone come to disturb them through the night. Once Andy awoke to hear a noise at a distance, but he soon figured out that this was nothing more than a hoot owl.

Ten o'clock of the next day found them on the river bank. They had brought their fishing tackle with them, and also an axe with which to chop some holes through the ice.

"Pretty thick, I'm thinking," announced Jack, as they came out on the ice. "We'll have our own troubles making holes."

"How foolish we were not to bring our skates along!" cried Randy. "We could have a dandy skate." Their skates had been left up at the Lodge.

"Never mind, we'll skate some other time," said Spouter. "We're out for some fish to-day."

Arthur M. Winfield

It took over half an hour to knock several fair-sized holes through the ice, and then the boys began their fishing, following directions that had been given to Gif by some of the older hunters.

"If I catch a whale I don't see how I'm going to bring him up through this hole," remarked Andy, with a grin.

"Oh, that's easy," returned his brother gayly. "All you'll have to do will be to jump in and push him up through the hole where I can get hold of him."

"Thank you, you can do the jumping in yourself. This water is about twenty degrees below Cicero."

"I was thinking that we could enlarge one of the holes and keep it open," said Jack, with a serious look on his face; "then all you fellows can come down here every morning and take a dip." At present they were obtaining water from a deep well directly outside of the kitchen.

They fished for a long time without getting even a nibble. But then Jack felt a gentle tug, and, after some little excitement, managed to bring out a fair-sized catch.

"Hurrah! The first fish!" he cried, holding it up proudly.

"And may he be the forerunner of many more," proclaimed Spouter.

"I want a whale," declared Randy.

Such a catch was an incentive to all of the others to do their best, and as a result inside of three hours the lads had eleven fish between them, some of fair size and others quite small, one, in fact, so tiny that it was thrown back into the stream, "so it might grow a little," as Fred expressed it.

"One o'clock!" announced Gif, looking at his watch. "I think we had better go back to the Lodge and have some of these fish fried for dinner."

"Second the commotion!" cried Randy quickly.

Properly fried, the freshly-caught fish proved delicious eating, and the boys lingered over the repast while a scrap of those which had been served was left. Half of the catch was packed away in snow to be served at another time.

The day had just come to an end when the boys heard a jingle of sleighbells on the road, and then came a whistle.

"It's Jed Wallop," announced Gif.

"Yes, and he's coming from the direction of Timminsport!" cried Fred. "He must have been down to the town."

"Look! He's holding up some letters!" ejaculated Jack. "Letters!"

"Letters! Letters!" was the general cry, and then the whole crowd of cadets rushed down to meet the old hunter.

CHAPTER XIX

LETTERS FROM HOME

While Gif was sorting out the mail, which included not only letters but also several packages which had been sent by parcel post, Jack and Spouter told the old hunter about the coming of the two bullies to the Lodge, and how they had sneaked away at daybreak.

"Accordin' to that, them fellers can't be very good friends o' yourn," remarked the old hunter dryly.

"They are our enemies," answered Spouter. "They did all sorts of mean things at Colby Hall, and when they were found out Werner got so scared that he ran away and never came back."

"I guess their folks ought to take 'em in hand. If they don't they'll be sorry fer it later on," said Wallop. "But I must be gittin' on now, fer I've got to git ready to-night fer a big day's work to-morrow."

"Some day we want you to come down here and go out hunting with us," said Jack. "Can't you show us where we can get a chance at a deer, or something else that is worth while?"

"Wot's the matter with stirrin' up a bear?" replied the old hunter, with a grin, his eyes twinkling.

"That would suit me to a T!" exclaimed Randy.

"Trot out your bears and we'll polish 'em off!" added his twin.

"Not many bears 'round here," announced Jed Wallop. "But you might strike something jest as bad, especially if the snow keeps on gittin' deeper. The wolves in this neighborhood git mighty pestiferous when they can't git nothin' to eat."

"Wolves!" exclaimed Fred. "Gee! I don't know that I want to run up against a savage wolf."

After promising to come down and see them during the following week, Jed Wallop drove off, leaving the boys to return to the Lodge and look over their letters and parcel post packages.

"Here is a letter from mother, and it encloses a letter from dad!" cried Jack, as he glanced over the epistle.

"I've got a letter from Mary," said Fred. "And here is one from May Powell, too."

"Who is your second letter from, Jack?" queried Spouter.

"Oh, never you mind about that."

"Looks as if it might be in Ruth Stevenson's handwriting," said Andy, with a grin.

There were letters for everybody. Two of the packages were from the Rover boys' homes, and the third had been sent to

Spouter by his mother.

"A fruit cake!" exclaimed Fred, as he opened the package addressed to him. "I'll tell you! It takes my mother to remember what us fellows like," and he smacked his lips.

The other package, addressed to Andy and Randy, contained a box of home-made sugar cookies, while that which Spouter had received contained a long loaf of ginger cake and a box of hard candies.

"Well, one thing is sure—they haven't forgotten us," was Spouter's remark, as he passed the candies around.

All the boys were anxious to read their letters, and for the time being everything else was forgotten. Mrs. Dick Rover wrote that nothing of importance had happened at home since they had gone away. Ruth Stevenson and May Powell were still with them, but all of the girls expected to go to the Stevenson homestead to finish their school vacation.

The letter from Dick Rover had been sent from the battlefront in France. In it he related how he and his brothers, as well as some of their old school chums, had been in a number of small engagements. In one of these Tom and Sam Rover had been slightly wounded by the fragments from a shell, and he himself had been in a gas attack, but had escaped without serious injury. All had been sent to the field hospital to be treated, but now they were once more at the front in what were called their winter quarters.

*   *   *   *   *

"The Boches are watching us like a cat watches a mouse, and we are equally on the alert," wrote Dick Rover. "There have been no big battles, but sniping is going on constantly, and several of our men have been killed or wounded. We are all anxious to have the cold weather break up, so that we can go forward and finish this war. We feel that we can wallop the enemy, if only we have a chance to get at them."

*   *   *   *   *

"That's dad, all right," murmured Jack admiringly. He had read the letter aloud for the benefit of the others.

"Oh, dear! I hope dad wasn't seriously hurt," murmured Fred.

"I think if our fathers were very badly hurt Uncle Dick would let us know," answered Randy. "He isn't one to hold back news—he knows we want the truth."

"If only this war was over!" remarked Andy, and now there was little of his usual light-heartedness in his tone. "I won't feel at ease until our soldiers are bound for home."

The six cadets talked over the letters they had received for some time. They had brought stationery with them, and they spent the evening writing letters in return.

"I don't see how we're going to get these down to Timminsport unless we walk down there," remarked Jack. "And a walk of five or six miles through this snow each way wouldn't be an easy job."

"I know what we can do," replied Gif. "We can skate down the river to a place called Henryville. There is a post-office there, and letters are sent over to Timminsport at least once a day."

"How far is it to Henryville?" questioned Randy.

"Oh, not more than three miles."

"Do you suppose the skating is any good?"

"I don't see why it shouldn't be."

"Let's do it!" broke in Spouter. "We wanted to have a skate anyway. We can take our guns along, in case we see any game." And so it was arranged.

The next day dawned bright and clear, and after breakfast the boys got their letters and their skates and started for the river.

"I'll wager we'll find the ice covered with snow in some places," remarked Randy.

"I don't know about that," answered Gif. "I was hoping the high wind had swept it pretty clean."

They were soon on the ice, their skates ringing merrily as they struck out into an impromptu race. They swept down the river and around a broad bend, and were soon well out of sight of the tract of forest land upon which the Lodge was located.

"I hope Glutts and Werner don't visit the bungalow during our absence," remarked Spouter.

"Well, that's a risk we've got to run," answered Jack. "We can't remain at home all the time."

"Exactly so!" put in Gif. "And it would be no fun for some of us to stay behind on guard while the others were off enjoying themselves."

For the most part they found the river swept clear of snow,

although here and there were drifts more or less deep over which they had to plough their way as best they could. This, however, was nothing but fun for the lads, and nobody complained.

Arriving at Henryville, they found that the mail for Timminsport would go out in less than an hour, and also learned that the mail from that place came in twice daily, morning and evening.

"Let's have all our mail re-addressed from Timminsport to Henryville," suggested Fred; "then we can come down here on our skates any time we feel like it and get it." And this was done.

They found a fairly good general store at Henryville, and made a few purchases of such things as they thought they could use to advantage during their outing. They were about to start up the river again when Jack's attention was attracted to a large sleigh drawn by a pair of powerful horses. The sleigh was driven by a man who looked as if he might be a German, and on the back seat, wedged in by a number of packages, were two other German-looking individuals.

"One of those men on the back seat is that Herman Crouse, the fellow we rescued from the burning car," said Jack to the others.

"Yes, and that driver and the other man are two of the fellows we met on the road when we were trying to locate the Lodge," added Randy.

"It's queer that that Herman Crouse should be up here," said Fred.

"Oh, I don't know. He said he worked a small farm

somewhere in this vicinity."

"I thought it was down near Enwood," remarked Spouter.

"One thing certain—I don't like the looks of those other Germans," came from Gif. "They look like mighty suspicious characters to me."

Even had the boys wished to do so, they got no opportunity to speak to the man they had rescued from the burning railroad car. The sleigh had stopped at a house in Henryville, and now it passed on around a corner of the road, and was soon lost to sight in the woods.

Now that they knew their letters were on the way, the cadets were in no hurry to get back to the Lodge. They had brought along a few sandwiches and now purchased some fresh doughnuts, in case they stayed away from the Lodge during the lunch hour.

"Let's take our time and skate up one or two branches of this river," suggested Gif. "It will be easier than walking, and we may have a chance at some game."

All were willing, and it was suggested that Gif led the way, which he did. They left the main stream and started up a smaller watercourse leading directly into the forest.

"I just saw a rabbit!" exclaimed Randy presently. "There he is now!" and, raising his gun, he fired quickly. But his aim was not good, and the bunny hopped behind a tree and out of sight.

"Too bad you had to take a shot for nothing," remarked Fred. "That may put the other game in this vicinity on the alert."

Soon they came to a point where skating was not so easy. At first they thought to go back, but then it was suggested that they tramp along the frozen-up watercourse on foot.

"I was thinking we might run across some brook mink up here," said Gif. "Or some ducks."

"Oh, I'd like to get a mink or a duck if there are any in this vicinity," answered Jack.

On they tramped until a good quarter of a mile had been covered. Then they caught sight of several rabbits, and brought down two of them. Later still they saw a squirrel, but though Spouter shot at the frisky creature, it managed to elude him.

"Well, we can't expect to bag everything we shoot at," consoled Jack.

"I think I know of a short cut from here to the Lodge," said Gif. "So if you would rather tramp through the woods than go back by way of the river, we might do so and get a chance at some other game."

"All right, Gif; lead the way," said Jack, and they went forward under Gif's guidance.

They were deep in the forest when they heard a whir overhead. They looked up quickly to see a number of partridges sailing past close to the tree tops.

"Quick!" yelled Jack, and blazed away, while all of the others did the same.

CHAPTER XX

LOST IN THE WOODS

There was no time wasted in shooting at the partridges which were flying along so close to the tree tops. The six cadets did their best but four of the charges went wild. The aim of Jack and Gif was effective, and one wounded partridge came fluttering down to the snow while another dropped dead on the branches of a nearby cedar.

"Hurrah! we've got two of them, anyhow," cried Gif, as he reached forward and quickly put the wounded bird out of its misery.

"We've got two provided we can reach that one up in the tree," answered Jack. "I'm afraid it's going to be some climb to get it down."

"That's so," said Randy.

"Oh, I can get up there in no time!" cried Andy gayly. "Here, take my gun," and with his usual agility he was soon mounting the branches of the big tree, taking particular delight in shaking down great masses of loose snow on the heads of those below.

As is usual with cedars, the branches were close together, and Andy soon found he would have his own troubles in reaching the point where the dead partridge rested. However, he kept on, worming his way upward as best he could, until he was within a few feet of the prize.

"Some climb, believe me!" he called out to those below. "This tree is almost as close-grown as a cedar bush."

Up went Andy, and presently managed to get hold of the dead partridge and drew the game toward him. Just as he did this he heard a peculiar sound a few feet below him on the other side of the tree.

"Hello! is somebody following me?" he questioned, looking down to see what the movement among the branches below meant.

There was no reply to his question, and Andy came to the conclusion that the branches must have become crossed in some way and then loosened themselves. He continued his descent, but just as he reached a branch two feet further down a peculiar cry came to his alert ears, a cry not unlike that of an angry cat.

"Hello! something is up in this tree, that is sure," he told himself.

He listened, and then heard another cry, this time less than two yards below him, coming from one of the larger branches of the big cedar. At once he sent up a shout.

"What's wanted?" questioned his twin. "Why don't you hurry up down so we can do some more hunting?"

"There is some wild animal in this tree!" answered Andy. "I

don't know what it is, but it sounds like a wildcat."

"A wildcat!" burst out several of the others.

"And Andy hasn't any gun!" cried Gif. "Come on, let us see if we can't shoot the thing!"

"Go slow there," cautioned Jack. "Let us see if we can't locate it and find out what it is first. We don't want it to attack Andy while he is unarmed."

"Are you in any danger, Andy?" called out Fred.

"Where is the cat—or whatever it is?" asked Randy.

"It's just below me somewhere. I can't see it, but I can hear it plainly enough. It's moving around in those lower branches. I guess I had better stay up here for a while;" and as he spoke Andy mounted to a higher limb. With no weapon handy, he had no desire to face any wild animal.

Those below slowly circled the big cedar, keeping their eyes on the alert for a view of whatever might be prowling around among the branches. They had their guns ready for use, but realized that they must fire with great caution, or otherwise they might hit the lad who was in peril.

"I suppose the wildcat, or whatever it is, was up in the tree and didn't know what to do when Andy started to come up. The beast knew we were down here, or otherwise it would probably have jumped down and run off."

"Squirrels don't cry like a cat, and I heard that beast just cry," said Jack. "All squirrels do is to chatter."

"There's another danger," said Gif. "If we come too close to that tree we'll probably drive the wildcat, or whatever it is, up to where Andy is."

"Here's the bird!" shouted Andy from above, and threw the partridge down and away from the tree.

Jack and Andy's twin took a few steps closer to the big cedar, at the same time holding their guns ready for instant use. They peered upward among the snow-laden branches, and presently caught sight of a slinking form resting in a crotch of the tree.

"There it is!" exclaimed Randy, and was on the point of firing when the wildcat—for such it had proved to be—dropped out of sight and leaped to a branch on the other side of the tree trunk.

"Hi there! don't drive that beast up here," called out Andy.

"Andy," called back his twin suddenly, "weren't you carrying that flashlight?"

"No, I left it at the Lodge. I didn't think I would want it on the trip to Henryville."

"I've got my flashlight," remarked Gif. "Here it is," and he brought it forth.

The light was flashed up into the tree and around from branch to branch. As the rays traveled through the cedar there was a sudden wild cry from the animal, and then came a swish and a whirr as the wildcat sprang to the outer end of a limb and then down into the snow.

Bang! bang! bang! went the guns in the hands of Gif, Randy, and Spouter. But whether they hit the wildcat or not, they could not tell. There was a whirl in the snow, and then in a twinkling the beast had disappeared into the forest behind them.

"Well, it's gone, anyhow," declared Jack, in a tone of great relief. "You can come down, Andy."

Andy was soon out of the tree, and, having picked up the two partridges, the six young hunters continued on their way, as they supposed, in the direction of Cedar Lodge.

Presently they came to another clearing, and on the far side of this noted some animals hopping about which they felt certain must be rabbits.

"Let's go over there!" cried Fred excitedly. "Maybe we can make a good haul."

"It's a pretty good tramp around to the other side of this clearing," remarked Gif. "And it looks to me as if it might begin to snow again," he added, with a glance at the sky which was now heavily overcast.

But all of the others wanted a chance to get more game, so in the end the six cadets tramped around one edge of the clearing until they reached a point close to the spot where the rabbits had been seen. Here the bunnies were out in force, trying to find something to eat, and they had but little difficulty in bagging four of the creatures.

"Well, that's not so bad but what it might be worse," announced Jack.

"We should have had more than four," grumbled Randy. "There were at least fifteen or sixteen rabbits to be seen." He had missed what he had thought to be a comparatively easy shot.

"Well, we can't have everything," declared Spouter philosophically.

They trudged on once more, Gif, as before, taking the lead. But presently the tall cadet called a halt.

"What's the matter now?" questioned Randy. "See any more game ahead?"

"No." Gif was staring around first to the right and then to the left. "Hang it if I know whether we are on the right trail or not!"

"Do you mean to say, Gif, you don't know in what direction the Lodge is located?" questioned Spouter quickly.

"I think it's off in that direction, Spouter," was the reply, and Gif pointed with his hand, "but I'm not dead sure of it. Circling that clearing threw me off the track."

"Well, were you sure of the trail before we came over here?" questioned Jack. "If you were, we can go back you know, even though it is quite a tramp."

"I thought I was sure, Jack. But now I'm not sure of anything," answered Gif helplessly. "Someway or other, I seem to be completely turned around."

"Gee! then we're in a pretty pickle," groaned Fred, who was beginning to grow tired of tramping through the snow.

"If we could only get down to the river again we'd be all right," came from Randy.

"I wonder if I could locate the Lodge from the top of one of these trees," remarked Jack. "It would be quite a climb to get such a view, but it would be better than tramping around without knowing where one was going."

"I'll do the climbing," answered Gif quickly. "I got you fellows into this mess, and it's up to me to get you out."

"Oh, don't think I'm complaining," returned Spouter quickly.

"None of us is complaining, Gif. We all know it's the easiest thing in the world to get lost in a big woods like this— especially when there is snow on the ground to cover up the landmarks."

A tall pine was selected, and the others boosted Gif upward as far as they could. Then he mounted from branch to branch, and the others waited below as patiently as possible for what he might have to report. In the meantime a few flakes of snow came drifting downward, and soon it was snowing steadily.

"Well, what can you see?" called out Jack, after those below had waited quite a while for their chum to make a report.

"I can't see very much on account of the snow coming down," announced Gif. "I can see the edge of a clearing that might be the one where Cedar Lodge is located, but I am not certain of it."

"Well, take another good look," advised Spouter. "Wish we had field glasses," he added.

It was a full fifteen minutes before Gif rejoined the others. He had located but one place that looked like the clearing surrounding the Lodge, but, as he had said before, he was by no means certain that this was the right location.

"Well, we might as well try it anyway," announced Jack. "We can't stay here all night."

"It's too bad it began to snow so heavily just as I was climbing the tree," remarked Gif. "If it hadn't been for that I might have gotten quite a view and maybe located the bungalow without difficulty. However, this may prove to be the right trail after all. Come on, before it gets dark."

"Wish I had something more to eat," remarked Andy. The few sandwiches and doughnuts they had brought along had long since been eaten.

As they walked on the way seemed to grow more difficult. They soon found themselves at a point where there were a series of rocks backed up by low-hanging bushes thickly covered with snow. There was no wind, but the snow was now coming down more thickly than ever.

"Gee! it looks to me as if we were lost," remarked Fred.

All gazed around them, but saw little to give them satisfaction. Behind them lay the thick forest, and in front of them the rocks and bushes. It was now growing dark, and this added to their uneasiness.

"Well, what shall we do next?" questioned Gif.

Nobody answered that question. They were undoubtedly lost, and what was to be done about it was a serious problem.

Arthur M. Winfield

CHAPTER XXI

A NIGHT UNDER THE CLIFF

"One thing is sure," said Jack presently. "We can't stand out here in this snowstorm all night."

"Let's go on at least a short distance further," broke in Spouter.

"Maybe we'll come to some sort of trail that Gif will recognize," put in Randy.

"I'm getting dead tired. I can't tramp more than a mile or two further," said Fred.

"I don't believe any of us care to go any such distance as that, Fred," returned Jack kindly. "Here, give me your gun. I'll carry it for you," for it was plainly to be seen the youngest Rover was becoming exhausted.

All were tired out from their skate and their tramp, and climbing among the rough rocks covered with snow was by no means easy.

Soon they reached another line of rocks, this time much higher than those they had been crossing. At one end of the rocks was a small cliff. At the top of this several cedars had once stood, but the winds of the winter before had blown them over, so that, while the roots were still imbedded in the cliff, the tops rested in the snow below.

"Great salt mackerel!" cried Gif in dismay. "Well, now I have spilled the beans!"

"What's up now?" questioned Randy quickly.

"I heard my uncle tell about this place. He visited it just after those trees fell over. He said the spot was about three miles from the Lodge."

At this there was a groan from the twins and Fred.

"We can't walk that distance in this snowstorm," said the latter decidedly.

"Not over those rough rocks, anyway," added Randy. "I feel as if my ankles were getting twisted out of shape."

"Do you know in what direction the Lodge is from here?" questioned Spouter.

"I do not, except that you have to be on the top of the cliff to get to it. We were evidently headed the right way, although we must have walked in a big semicircle since we left the river."

"I'm going to climb to the top of the cliff and have a look around," declared Jack. "Here, take these guns and the game."

It was no easy matter to mount to the top of the cliff which at this point was at least fifteen feet over their heads. But Jack finally made it, and was followed by Spouter and Gif.

Here, however, the view was no better than from below—the thickly falling snow hiding the landscape on every side. Night was coming on and it was growing colder, and the boys could not help but shiver.

"I guess the best thing we can do it to try to make ourselves comfortable for the night," remarked Jack.

"How can we make ourselves comfortable without anything to eat?" questioned Spouter.

"We've got the game. We can start a fire and cook some of that."

"And besides, you must remember we have the things we bought at Henryville," said Gif.

The three rejoined the others, and the question of what to do was put to the younger Rovers. Fred and Andy declared they could not tramp much further, and at once agreed that it would be best to try to make themselves comfortable for the night.

"It looks as if there might be some kind of shelter under those fallen cedars," said Randy. "Hanging down from the top of the cliff, they form a sort of lean-to."

"I was thinking of that," said Jack. "Let us get under them and investigate."

"Beware of more wildcats," cautioned Andy.

"We'll use my flashlight," said Gif.

This was done, he and several of the others investigated the spot under the fallen cedars with care. No trace of any wild animal, not even a rabbit or a squirrel, was found. Then the boys began to size up the situation, trying to determine how they could make themselves at home there for the night.

"First of all I think we had better build a fire," suggested Gif. "Then, after we have warmed up and rested a bit, we can prepare supper."

With so much wood at hand it was an easy matter to start a campfire. This was placed at one side of the opening under the fallen cedars, the boys taking care that the flames should not reach the trees. With their hatchet they cut off some of the cedar boughs and scattered these over the ground for a flooring. The driest they placed to one side to use for bedding later.

Fortunately while at Henryville they had purchased a fair-sized box of cocoa. This box was of tin, and Jack suggested that they dump the cocoa out on a sheet of paper which he had in his pocket and then use the tin for a pot in which to boil water.

"It won't make a very large cocoa pot, but it will be better than nothing, and we can fill it as many times as we please."

The boys had several collapsible drinking cups with them, and these they would take turns in using.

"I'm mighty glad we bought that cheese," remarked Spouter. "That will help out quite a little," for they carried a piece weighing almost two pounds.

Of the other things purchased at Henryville, only a box of fancy crackers could be used. There were two dozen all told,

Arthur M. Winfield

and these were divided by Randy, four crackers to each cadet.

"We'll clean a couple of the rabbits and see what we can do about broiling them over the flames," said Gif. "Now you fellows can show what you can do," he added, with a grin. "It's all well enough to work when you've got the tools to work with, but quite another story when you've got next to nothing."

Water was obtained by melting a quantity of the snow, and soon they had the first can of hot cocoa ready. In the meanwhile several of the lads were broiling the rabbits as best they could.

"I know how I'm going to heat the next can of water," declared Andy. "I'm going to do as the Indians did—drop a clean, redhot stone into it." And this he did later on and got his boiling water in short order.

It was not a very satisfactory meal, but the lads had fun eating it, and they did not complain when they found portions of the broiled rabbits slightly burnt and found that four fancy crackers with cheese each did not take the place of a big pan of biscuits or a good-sized loaf of bread.

"One thing is in our favor, anyhow," said Fred, with a sigh of satisfaction, after they had finished their scant meal. "We won't have to wash the dishes."

The can was dried over the fire, the cocoa was replaced, and then the lads proceeded to make themselves comfortable for the night. They missed their blankets, and it was therefore decided that they should take turns in sitting up and guarding the fire, so that all might keep warm without running the danger of setting fire to the cedars under which they were resting.

It proved to be a long and wearisome night for most of them. The resting places were anything but soft, and a fitful wind often blew the smoke of the campfire toward the would-be sleepers, causing them to cough and shift their positions. But neither man nor beast came to disturb them, for which they were thankful.

"Going to bother about breakfast?" questioned Jack, as he sat up and saw that Gif and Spouter were already stirring.

"I don't think so," was the answer. "If you fellows are willing, we'll strike right out for the Lodge. We can get a better meal there."

The others agreed, and almost before daylight they were on their way again. They climbed to the top of the cliff, and, after moving around cautiously for several hundred feet, reached a well defined trail running in the direction Gif thought they ought to take.

The storm had cleared away, and soon the sun came peeping over the treetops.

"Gee! I won't do a thing to a good hot breakfast when we reach the Lodge," remarked Randy to his twin.

"I'll be with you," returned Andy. "A big heaping plate of pancakes with maple syrup for me, flanked by a couple of good-sized sausage cakes and washed down with a big cup of that cocoa!"

"Say, Andy, you make me hungry clean down to my shoes!" burst out Fred.

"I think we'll all be able to eat a good breakfast by the time we get there," announced Gif.

Arthur M. Winfield

"Are you sure you are on the right trail, Gif?" questioned Spouter anxiously.

"Yes, I know where I am now. It's queer how I got mixed up before."

"How much further?" questioned Jack.

"About half a mile."

They crossed another small clearing, and on the edge of this caught sight of several more rabbits. Jack and Randy fired simultaneously and were lucky to bring down two of the bunnies.

"They will help out the larder just so much more," announced Gif, after they had tried for several minutes to stir up more of the rabbits, but without success.

"I wish we could get a chance at some other kind of game," remarked Jack.

Presently they caught sight of Cedar Lodge at a distance, and then all hurried their pace.

"Looks mighty good to a fellow after he's been away all night," declared Spouter.

"Look, Look!" burst out Gif. "What can that mean? Every window and every door of the Lodge is wide open!"

"Sure as you're born, Gif is right!" ejaculated Fred. "Something is wrong, that's sure."

All set off on a run, to ascertain as quickly as possible what had occurred at the Lodge during their absence. Gif was the first to enter the place, but he was quickly followed by the others.

"Gee! what do you know about this?" ejaculated Andy.

"This is the work of our enemies!" murmured Jack.

The doors and windows had evidently been open for some time, for the Lodge was bitter cold inside and not a little snow had drifted in through the openings. The wind had likewise entered, blowing the ashes of the dead fire in all directions.

"I'll bet Glutts and Werner did this!" cried Spouter.

"Just what I think," answered Jack.

Arthur M. Winfield

CHAPTER XXII

AT TONY DUVAL'S CAMP

The six cadets lost no time in making a thorough examination of the Lodge. In the bedrooms they found everything
topsy-turvy, the bed clothes having been hauled near the
windows where the incoming snow might fall upon them. In
the kitchen they found many of their cooking utensils in the
sink, and over them had been poured a mixture of flour,
catsup, maple syrup, and condensed milk. In the storeroom
many other things were upset, and not a few of the supplies
appeared to be missing.

"This is certainly the worst yet!" groaned Fred, as he looked
at the mussed-up and ruined food.

"I said Glutts and Werner would get back at you for
meddling with their supplies," remarked Jack sharply. "They
have certainly paid us back with interest."

"I wish we had those two fellows here now. I'd hammer them
good and proper," declared Randy. "Just the same, I suppose
this is our fault, and I'm mighty sorry for it," he added,
looking at Jack, Gif, and Spouter.

"They either took a large share of our supplies away, or else hid them," said Gif, after another look around. "My, what a mess they did make!"

"Well, as we are largely responsible for this, it's up to us to take hold and clean up the best we can," announced Randy to his twin and Fred.

"Right you are," answered Andy. "Come ahead! we'll clean up the living-room first and get a fresh fire started."

"All right, you fellows do that, and we'll tackle the bedrooms," said Jack. "We'll have to dry out that bedding before night."

Soon the whole crowd was busy, breakfast, for the time, being forgotten. All went at the task with a will, and before long everything was straightened out but the kitchen. Doors and windows had been closed, a fresh fire had been lit, and then the roaring logs sent a grateful warmth through the entire bungalow.

"Now we'll get breakfast, and then we'll clean up this mess in the kitchen," announced Gif.

"And what are we going to do after that?" questioned Jack.

"What do you think we ought to do, Jack?"

"Square accounts with Glutts and Werner, if they are the guilty parties."

"They only paid us back for what Fred and the twins did," said Spouter. "I don't know but what we might as well call it quits."

"Well, we'll go over there, anyway, and see what they've got to say for themselves," said Jack. "Perhaps at the least we'll be able to scare them so that they'll leave us alone in the future."

"All right, we might do that," answered Gif; and so it was decided.

The boys came to the conclusion that Glutts and Werner, accompanied possibly by Codfish, must have visited the Lodge some time in the middle of the previous afternoon. Evidently the marauders had been afraid that the bungalow's occupants might return at any moment, for they had worked with great speed.

"They took a big chance with that fire," remarked Randy. "If the wind had blown the sparks too far—into the bedrooms for instance—the whole place might have gone up in flames."

At first the lads thought to go over to Tony Duval's place without delay. But by the time they had straightened out the bungalow and gotten their breakfast, the older cadets were in a different frame of mind.

"More than likely they'll be on their guard to-day, looking for us to come over," said Jack. "Let us wait two or three days and try to catch them unawares," and this change was made in their plans.

Several days, including Sunday, passed, and the six cadets took it easy. It snowed part of the time, so that they went out hunting only once. On that trip they managed to get several more rabbits and four quail, but that was all.

"I thought I saw a fox," said Gif on the morning following. "I heard him bark during the night too."

"Was he a silver fox?" questioned Jack eagerly.

"I didn't see him well enough to find out, and I can't tell the color of a fox from his bark," was Gif's somewhat dry reply. And at this there was a laugh.

Then the storm cleared away once more, and on the following morning the boys resolved to tramp in the direction of Tony Duval's place and see if they could locate Werner and Glutts.

"I don't believe this Tony Duval is a very nice fellow to meet," remarked Gif, when they were on their way. "I saw him twice, and he looked like anything but a pleasant character."

The middle of the forenoon found them on the grounds occupied by the various shacks belonging to the French-Canadian. They were small structures, built for the most part of slabsides, and each contained but two windows and a door.

"I wonder which shack is that used by Glutts and Werner," remarked Randy, as they looked around.

Nobody was in sight. There were five of the shacks located several hundred feet apart, and each with some timber around it.

"We'll try the nearest place," said Gif, and, going up to it, he knocked sharply on the door. He waited for fully a minute, but there was no reply.

"Seems to be empty," remarked Jack, after looking in through one of the windows. "There is no sign of a fire in the fireplace."

They tramped on to the next shack, and found that was likewise vacant.

"I think we'll find somebody at home in the third shack," announced Spouter. "Anyway, I see smoke coming from the chimney."

They were approaching the doorway of this rude structure when it was suddenly flung open and a man stepped into view. He wore a hunter's outfit, and carried a double-barreled shotgun in his hands.

"Who are you?" he questioned, and his tone had a strong French accent. "What do you want here?"

"We are looking for a fellow named Werner who hired one of these shacks," answered Gif.

"Who are you?" repeated the man sharply, and then Gif recognized Tony Duval.

"I am the son of one of the men who own Cedar Lodge. We want to find Werner and the two fellows who are with him."

"Aha! So you are the young fellows from Cedar Lodge who made so much trouble for Mistaire Werner and his friends," cried Tony Duval. "He has told me all about that."

"Did he tell you what he did down at Cedar Lodge?" demanded Jack.

"He say he would square the account. Why should he not do that? You have no right to destroy his things and hurt his horse."

"We didn't touch his horse!" answered Fred quickly.

"His horse is gone lame, and he say you do that," cried Tony Duval. "I do not want such people as you around my place. You can go back, and you must stay off my property," and Tony Duval emphasized his words by handling his shotgun suggestively.

"If Werner and his friend are here we want to see them," cried Jack sharply. "Which shack do they live in?"

"They live there." Duval pointed with his thumb. "They are not at home now. They go on a hunt. But you shall not make more trouble for them or you will hear from me," and again he handled his gun suggestively. The man's face was very red and looked as if he had been drinking. Evidently he was in an ugly humor.

After that the cadets attempted to argue with Tony Duval, but all to no purpose. He was very stubborn, and he insisted upon it that they had already made a great deal of trouble for his patrons. He finally ordered them away, and acted so threateningly that they retired.

"Well, we've had our walk for nothing," remarked Fred, when they were in the woods again.

"I don't know about that," answered Randy. "Let us keep our eyes open. Maybe we'll run across Werner and Glutts."

The four Rovers and their chums walked leisurely through the woods, keeping their eyes open for the possible appearance of their enemies, and also for any game that might present itself. Thus the best part of an hour went by, and they managed to bring down one more rabbit and also a squirrel. Then they heard some shooting at a distance, and walked cautiously in that direction.

"There they are!" cried Randy presently, and pointed out of the woods and across a small clearing.

All looked in the direction indicated, and there saw Werner, Glutts, and Codfish. Each had a gun, and the three had been shooting at a number of rabbits. Only Werner had been successful, the others shooting wide of the mark.

"Let us circle the clearing and surprise them," said Jack, and to this the others immediately agreed.

With caution they made their way around the clearing, doing their best to remain hidden from the other boys. They had no desire to be mistaken for game and shot at, so they had to keep their eyes on the alert as they advanced.

Werner and his cronies had passed into the woods, and now were making their way down a hillside into a hollow where they had built a fair-sized campfire. As the Rovers and their chums came closer they saw the three sitting around the campfire and evidently getting ready to have a midday lunch.

"Come on! We're six to three, so we ought to be able to manage those fellows with ease!" cried Fred.

"Wait a minute! I've got an idea!" exclaimed Randy, holding his cousin back.

"What is it?" questioned Spouter.

"Do you see how much higher the other side of the slope is?" went on Andy. "Well, that slope runs right down to where they are sitting and have their fire. Now a few big snowballs started down that slope—"

"I've got you, Andy!" burst out his twin, with twinkling eyes. "It will be great! Come on, fellows, we'll smother 'em with snow!"

Arthur M. Winfield

CHAPTER XXIII

SIX BIG SNOWBALLS

It did not take the four Rovers and their chums long to reach that part of the slope pointed out by Andy. As he had said, this was much higher than the spot where they had stood before and the slope was much steeper, leading directly down to where Werner, Glutts, and Codfish were now busy over their campfire preparing the midday meal.

The bully and his cronies were good feeders, and had brought a considerable quantity of food for their lunch. Some of this was now spread out on a napkin resting on the snow, and the rest of it was being warmed over the campfire.

"It's the chance of our lives," said Randy softly. "Come on, fellows, let's make the biggest snowballs we can."

All of the others were willing, and soon they had rolled six snowballs, each of which was two feet or more in diameter.

Of course, our friends were well out of sight of those in the hollow, and as they spoke in low tones their enemies had no suspicion of what was coming.

"Now then, place all the snowballs in a line on the very edge of the slope," said Jack. "And, Gif, you give the word when we are to push them down."

Soon the six massive snowballs were lined up side by side. Those behind them looked below to make sure that none of the trio was close to the fire, because they did not wish anybody to be burnt.

"Now then," whispered Gif suddenly, when he saw the three lads sit down with the cooked stuff between them. "All ready? Go!"

Everybody gave a shove, and over the edge of the slope went the six snowballs, slowly at first, but gradually gathering both size and speed. Through the snow they rolled and over the bare rocks until almost to the foot of the slope.

"Hi! what's this coming?" roared Glutts, happening to glance around as a strange noise reached his ears.

"It's a snowslide!" screamed Werner.

"Oh, oh! let me get out of the way!" shrieked Codfish.

All three attempted to spring to their feet, Glutts knocking over a pot of hot coffee as he did so. But the movement came too late, for the next instant the six snowballs bowled over the three boys, hurling them in all directions. One ball rolled through the lunch, carrying most of this along, imbedded in the snow. Another snowball went directly through the campfire, smashing that flat and leaving the embers hissing and blackened.

"Don't let them see you," called Jack, as the twins were about to dash down the slope. "Get back there out of sight."

"Oh, they'll know we did it, all right enough," answered Spouter. "Come on down and have it out with them."

This was what the majority desired, and before Glutts and the others could recover from their astonishment and dismay Gif and his crowd were down the slope.

"Huh! so you were the fellows to roll those snowballs down on us," growled Bill Glutts, as he rubbed his leg where some of the hot coffee had been spilled upon it.

"That's a fine way to treat a fellow," said Werner, digging some snow from his ear.

"And you spoiled all the lunch!" wailed Codfish, looking around for his cap, which had been knocked off. "Oh dear! I wish I hadn't come to this out-of-the-way place!"

"Shut up your whining!" roared Werner. "You make me sick!"

"I don't care. I told you yesterday I wanted to go home," answered Codfish complainingly. "I hate it up here!"

"Well, go home then!" snapped Werner. "Go home this minute if you want to. I'm sick of having you around."

"You'd do much better, Codfish, if you wouldn't train with fellows like Werner and Glutts," remarked Jack.

"If I leave them will you fellows show me the way back to Timminsport?" questioned the sneak of Colby Hall pleadingly. It was plainly to be seen that he had had no easy time of it since he had come up into the woods.

"That depends," said Gif, and caught the youth by the wrist.

"Tell me, Codfish, were you at our Lodge the other day—the day the whole place was rough-housed?"

"No, I wasn't, Gif. Really and truly I wasn't!" cried the sneak, in alarm.

"Were Werner and Glutts alone?"

"Yes, yes! I had nothing to do with it!"

"See here, Codfish, you keep your mouth shut!" roared Glutts, and he moved forward as if to strike the small youth who cowered before him.

"You keep your distance, Glutts," admonished Jack. "If Codfish is tired of staying with you fellows, he's going to leave, and you're not to say anything about it."

"What right had you fellows to smash those snowballs down on us?" questioned Werner, with an angry look in his eyes.

"What right had you fellows to come and upset Cedar Lodge, destroying some of our stores, and walking off with some of the others?" questioned Jack sternly.

"We didn't walk off with anything," answered Werner quickly. "What we did we had a right to do—to pay you back for what you did to our stores in the sleigh."

"We didn't take any of your things," put in Fred quickly; "and a whole lot of our stuff is missing."

"We didn't take a thing away—not a thing," put in Glutts, and he smiled grimly to himself as he spoke.

"I know what they did!" cried Codfish quickly. "If you'll take me along with you, and see that I get to Timminsport safely, I'll tell you where your things are."

"You say a word, Codfish, and I'll lambaste the life out of you!" yelled Werner.

"You won't touch Codfish!" broke in Jack sturdily. "And if he wants to go with us, he'll go."

"I want to go!" wailed the sneak. "I don't want to stay with them another minute. But how am I to get my things that are up at their shack?" he questioned helplessly.

"Well go up there with you," answered Gif.

A war of words followed, and then in uncontrolled rage Werner and Glutts attacked Jack and Gif. Half a dozen blows were exchanged, and then Glutts attempted to run away while Werner attempted to use the butt of his gun as a club. Andy tripped Glutts up, and Spouter caught Werner from behind, and as a consequence of the general mix-up the two bullies received a well-deserved drubbing. Then their weapons were discharged and their ammunition was taken away from them, and they were told to march back to Tony Duval's shacks.

Here, as they expected, our friends had another set-to with the French-Canadian. Tony Duval wanted to take sides with Werner and Glutts, but the others would not listen.

"This young man is going with us, and he is going to take his things with him," announced Gif, pointing to Codfish. "If you make any trouble for us, Duval, I'll at once notify my father and my uncle, and likewise the authorities at Portview. Your reputation around here is already none of the best, and I'll see to it that you are treated as you deserve."

"Bah! what do I care for you or your father or your uncle?" cried Tony Duval, in a rage. "This is my property. You will leave it at once."

"We'll leave when this young man has his things, and not before," answered Jack, and now he, too, fingered his gun in a suggestive manner.

Tony Duval realized that he was outnumbered and that the boys from Cedar Lodge meant business. He grumbled a good deal and talked in a whisper with Werner and Glutts. In the meanwhile, Codfish hurriedly gathered together his few belongings, and presently announced that he was ready to leave.

"Now, one thing more," said Gif, turning to the two bullies. "Don't you dare to show your faces anywhere near Cedar Lodge again. If you come on our property, you come at your own peril."

"Oh, you don't know how to take a joke," grumbled Glutts.

"We'll do as we please," added Werner, but it was plainly to be seen that he was much disturbed.

The boys were about ready to leave the shack when they heard the sound of sleigh bells, and soon a two-seated sleigh came into sight drawn by a pair of powerful horses. The turnout drove directly to the front of the shack occupied by Tony Duval.

"Hello! there are those men again," cried Gif.

All looked and saw that he referred to the Germans they had met on the road when looking for Cedar Lodge. The newcomers paid no attention to them, but leaped out of the sleigh and entered the Duval shack.

"I must go," said Tony Duval abruptly. "And I want you to go, too, and never come back here again," he added, and then hurried away.

"Who are those men?" questioned Jack, turning to Werner and Glutts.

"That's none of your business," answered Werner sourly. "You clear out of here and never come back."

There seemed nothing to do but to leave the premises, yet the Rovers and their chums were curious to know who the Germans were and what their errand to Tony Duval's shack could be. Yet they had no excuse for lingering longer, so presently they took their departure, Werner and Glutts looking sourly after them as they walked away.

"Do you know, I'd give a good deal to know more about those Germans," remarked Jack, as they trudged along. "I wonder what they want here? They can't be hunters, because they haven't any hunting outfits."

"They certainly couldn't be up here for business," returned Spouter, "because there is no business to speak of in this vicinity. Why, there isn't even a farm or a farmer around here, and the nearest logging camp is miles away, so they told me at Henryville."

"I'll tell you what we might do," said Gif. "We might pass into the woods and then turn around and come back again up behind Tony Duval's shack. We can watch and see what the Germans do, and maybe we'll hear what they and Duval have to say."

"That's an idea!" cried Jack. "I don't know but what we had better act on it."

Arthur M. Winfield

CHAPTER XXIV

A CONVERSATION OF IMPORTANCE

"Do you know anything about those Germans?" questioned Fred, turning to Codfish.

"I know they came to see Tony Duval once or twice before," answered the sneak of Colby Hall. "They and Duval seem to have some secret business between them."

"Do you know what it is?" asked Jack.

At this Codfish shook his head.

"Did Werner and Glutts have anything to do with it?" came from Gif.

"They went to Duval's cabin once when the Germans were there. I asked to go along, but they wouldn't let me. After that Bill and Gabe took some kind of a message down to Timminsport for them. It was on their way back from the town that they stopped and made a mess of things at your Lodge. They were laughing and joking about it when they got back, and that is how I know what took place."

"You said you would tell us where the things that were taken away are," came from Spouter.

"They are all in the barn under the hay—at least that is what Bill and Gabe said. They took 'em out there in one of the bed sheets."

"I guess that's right," came quickly from Gif. "I noticed that one of the sheets was missing."

They had now reached the shelter of the forest, and here, after a little talk, it was decided that the twins and Fred should return to Cedar Lodge at once, taking Codfish with them, while Jack, Gif, and Spouter took a roundabout course leading to the rear of Tony Duval's shack.

"We've got to be careful," announced Jack. "For all we know, those Germans may be desperate characters."

"And on the other hand they may be the most innocent fellows in the world," added Spouter. "Remember, not all the German-Americans in this country are unpatriotic."

The three soon reached a point where they could catch sight of Duval's shack. They approached with caution so that they might not be seen from the single back window of which the rough building boasted. As the boys drew closer they saw that the window had been raised several inches. Evidently there was a good fire going inside of the shack, and with so many occupants the place had become overly warm.

"Then it's all settled, and you'll attend to the matter?" they heard one of the Germans remark, as they crawled up close to the building.

"Yes, I'll do it," answered Tony Duval. "But I'll be running a big risk."

"Not if you are careful," said another of the Germans.

"And don't forget that you are being well paid for your work," added a third German, "and that you are doing this for the country in which your mother was born."

"I should not want to be caught," grumbled Tony Duval. "If I was, the authorities might hang me."

"Poof! be not so chicken-hearted," said the German who had first spoken. "Now it is all arranged, be careful that you do not disappoint us," he added sternly.

The three cadets had listened to this talk with intense interest. Now Jack could not resist the temptation to peer in at one corner of the window. He saw one of the Germans returning a wallet to his pocket, and saw Tony Duval take up several bank bills from the table and place them away in his hunting jacket. All of the Germans were on their feet, and now turned to the door, which one of them flung wide open.

"It's all over; get back as far as you can to the woods," whispered the oldest Rover boy, and led the way with the others at his heels.

When the cadets gained the shelter of the trees they saw the Germans get into the sleigh once more, and a few seconds later they drove away, Tony Duval watching their departure.

"Now what do you make of that, Jack?" questioned Gif. His face showed that he was puzzled.

"It looks to me as if those fellows were up to no good," returned Jack.

"Did you notice what they said about Tony Duval's mother?"

cried Spouter. "That seemed to me as if his mother might have been a German woman."

"That's the way I took it, too," returned Jack. "And then, don't forget what Duval said—that the authorities might hang him if he was caught. That sounds as if they were asking him to do something which was against the law."

"Yes, and a big crime at that," put in Gif.

"I wonder where the Germans live?"

"Most likely at a distance. Otherwise they wouldn't be using a sleigh."

"We ought to look into this, and without delay," said Jack decidedly.

"Let us make it our business to find out all about the Germans to-morrow," said Gif. And so it was decided.

When the three arrived at Cedar Lodge they found the others were already there and had uncovered the goods hidden by Glutts and Werner under the hay in the barn. There they likewise found the bedsheet and the blanket which had previously been taken.

"Well, anyway, they didn't rob us," was Randy's comment.

"I guess they were afraid to do that," answered his twin. "They thought we might bring the law down on them."

"I don't like those fellows any more, and I intend to have nothing more to do with 'em," said Codfish.

"I guess they got you up here simply to make you toady

to them."

"That's what they did, Andy. They made me carry all the things for 'em, and made me cut the wood and wash the dishes and everything. I was a big fool to leave home, where I might have had a splendid time during the holidays."

That evening came the first real drawback of the outing. In returning from the barn Spouter slipped on some ice and fell down with his foot under him. When he got up he found that his ankle was sprained, so that he could scarcely walk upon it. The others assisted him into the bungalow and did what they could to make him comfortable.

"I guess I'll be all right in a day or two," grumbled Spouter. "But this will prevent me from going out with you to-morrow to find out about those Germans."

"Well, anyway, Spouter, you'll have Codfish here to keep you company, and I'm sure he'll be glad enough to get something to eat for you," said Jack.

"I'll do that willingly if only you won't call me Codfish any more," pleaded the cadet mentioned.

"All right, Henry. We'll have to call you by your right name after this." And at this the sneak of the school seemed much relieved. Secretly, he hated the nickname of Codfish exceedingly.

Early in the morning came a surprise. The boys heard a well-known whistle and beheld Jed Wallop approaching, this time on foot. The old hunter had his gun with him.

"Thought I'd make a day of it with you," he announced. "That is, unless you've some other plans."

"We were thinking of coming over to your place," answered Jack. "We want to get some information."

"All right. I'm the walkin' dictionary and cyclopaedia of this hull district," answered Jed Wallop, with a grin. "Go on and fire all the questions at me that you want to."

The old hunter listened with interest to what the cadets had to say concerning the Germans and Tony Duval, and also about the message Glutts and Werner had carried to Timminsport for the strangers.

"That don't look right to me, at all," he said, shaking his head gravely. "I've seen them Germans a few times myself, drivin' around in that big sleigh of theirn. Sometimes there's only two of 'em, and then agin the four are in a bunch. Someone once told me that Duval had German blood in his veins, and I guess that's right."

"And I'm sure Glutts is German, and maybe Werner too," said Randy.

"My idee is that them Germans are holdin' out at an old house up River Bend way. It was the old Parkingham estate, but it hasn't been used for years. It's a mighty lonely place, too, right in the midst of the woods."

"How far is that from here?" questioned Fred.

"About three miles, I should say."

"Is there a pretty good road?" questioned Jack.

"The way by the mountain road would be all of five miles. But I know a fair trail through the woods that we might take."

Arthur M. Winfield

"Then let's get there as soon as possible!" cried Gif. "Will you go with us, Jed?"

"O' course I will! If them Germans are traitors to this country, or anything like that, I want to know it," answered the old hunter decidedly. "I'm too old to enlist for the war, but I ain't too old to do my duty by Uncle Sam."

"We might combine business with pleasure," remarked Jack. "We can take our guns and game bags, and also a substantial lunch. Then if we see any signs of game going or coming, we can take our time about getting back here."

"One thing that brought me over was this," went on Jed Wallop. "I heard one of you young fellers sayin' you wanted to get a crack at a silver fox. Well, I know a holler about two miles from here where quite a few foxes are hangin' out. I've heard 'em barkin' around there more than once. I saw a silver fox up that way, too, and if he shows himself you might git what you are wishin' fer."

"Fine!" exclaimed Jack, with enthusiasm. "But is that hang-out of the foxes on the way to the old mansion you mentioned?"

"No, it ain't. But we might work around that way comin' back."

A substantial lunch was prepared and packed, and then, after seeing to it that their guns were in good order, the five cadets and Jed Wallop left the Lodge.

"Mighty sorry I can't go along," said Spouter dolefully. "However, I wish you all the best of luck, not only in getting some information about those Germans, but also in locating the foxes."

"And you can depend on me taking good care of Dick," said Henry Stowell.

"All right, Henry," answered Gif; for he and all of the others had been told how Codfish hated his nickname, and they had decided to do what they could toward dropping it, although, as Andy had remarked, "It might be pretty hard to stop calling a donkey a donkey all the time."

"We'll give the little sneak a chance to turn over a new leaf," was what Jack had said in return. "I don't believe Codfish is bad at heart—he's only been traveling in the wrong company."

It was a fair day with the sun coming up clearly over the treetops. It was still intensely cold, but there was little or no wind, for which the lads were thankful.

"I suppose you have thinned out the game a good deal right around this Lodge," remarked Jed Wallop. "You know rabbits and squirrels don't like to hear the bangin' of a gun. They know mighty well it spells trouble fer 'em."

A mile was covered before they sighted anything that looked like game. Then a big fat rabbit ran directly across their path. To give the boys a chance, Jed Wallop did not fire, and as a consequence the bunny got away, none of the cadets being quick enough to get a shot at it.

"You've got to have your eyes open if you want to lay low all the game in these woods," chuckled the old hunter.

"He was too close to us," grumbled Gif. "Why, he was out of sight before I could think of raising my gun!"

"You mustn't think, Gif. Jest fire and let it go at that," and

Arthur M. Winfield

Jed Wallop grinned broadly. He was a man who loved company, and he thought it great sport to be out in the woods with the cadets.

After this they trudged along in silence, each of the lads keeping his eyes wide open for the possible appearance of any game. But nothing came to view.

"Now we'll soon be in sight of that old house," announced Jed Wallop presently. "It's on the other side of this hill."

They topped the rise, and there saw before them a small clearing, beyond which was a rough mountain road. On the other side of the road was a thick patch of timber, and in the midst of this stood a long low house with a wide veranda in front.

"There is the Parkingham house," said Jed Wallop. "And unless I'm greatly mistaken that's where them Germans are hangin' out."

CHAPTER XXV

TEE MYSTERIOUS HOUSE IN THE WOODS

"We don't want anyone to see us," remarked Jack, as they came to a halt on the edge of the clearing.

"Oh, them Germans won't know but what you're simply out huntin'," answered Jed Wallop.

Nevertheless, the boys were anxious to approach the old house unobserved, and so skirted the clearing and crossed the mountain road, which at this point was lined with thick pines. Then they entered the forest again, coming up presently at a point in the rear of the building where there was a small barn and also several sheds.

The Parkingham house was a rambling structure which had seen better days. One end sagged, and here a porch post had fallen away, along with several steps. But the other end of the long building had evidently been put in some kind of repair, for some boards on the piazza were new, as were also several window sashes. All the curtains were drawn down.

"Somebody mast be living here," remarked Randy. "Otherwise they wouldn't have gone to the trouble and expense of making repairs."

Arthur M. Winfield

They looked around the old house carefully, but could see nobody. Then they peered into the barn.

"No horses here," announced Gif. "And that big sleigh isn't here either."

"Then, if those Germans live here, they must be away on a trip," remarked Jack after a pause.

"I don't see anything suspicious around this place," said Andy.

The barn showed signs of use, and so did the other outbuildings, and there were numerous tracks in the snow leading from the barn to the house. At the well some water had been spilled, and this had not yet had time to freeze.

"They can't have gone away so very long ago," was Gif's comment. He turned to the others. "Well, what's the next move?"

"I don't see why you don't walk right up and knock on the door, and if them fellers are around have a talk with 'em," declared Jed Wallop. "If they are above board, they won't hesitate about answerin' questions."

"Let us wait around the barn for a while and see if anybody comes in or goes out," suggested Jack. He could not get it out of his mind how queerly the Germans had acted, and he felt certain that something was wrong and that the fellows ought to be reported to the authorities.

"Gee! it's rather cold around here," remarked Fred, as they walked up and down in the big barn to keep warm.

"I'm going to cover myself in the hay if you fellows are

going to stay here any length of time," cried Andy, and in a playful mood he and his twin made a dash for what looked to be a large quantity of hay at one side of the barn. Both burrowed down in this, and then Randy set up a cry of surprise.

"Hello! this isn't a pile of hay at all. It's bundles of wire!"

"Bundles of wire?" queried Jack.

"What kind of wire?" asked Gif.

"Looks like fence wire, or telegraph wire, to me," said Andy, who was holding some of the hay to one side so that he might get a better look at what was underneath. "It looks brand new, too."

There were numerous coils of the wire, and these the cadets and Jed Wallop looked at with interest. Then they found several packing cases, all nailed up tightly and marked in English and in German.

"This is certainly queer," said Jack.

"Say, what's the matter with opening one or two of the cases and seeing what's in 'em?" suggested Fred.

"Have we any right to do that?" asked Gif doubtfully.

"We'll take the right," decided Jack. "I'm satisfied that those fellows are up to no good. You know what Tony Duval said when they asked him to do something."

Not far from the barn was a woodshed, and here the cadets procured an axe and a hammer. With these implements they managed to pry open one of the packing cases. Inside was what looked to be electrical machinery, but just what it was they could not make out.

"Looks like that telephone or telegraph line all right enough," remarked Randy. "But what are those fellows going to do with any such line as that away up here?"

"It's a riddle, ain't it?" remarked Jed Wallop. "Jest the same, that stuff looks mighty suspicious to me."

They continued their investigation, and behind the packing cases found some machinery. All of it was new and strange to them.

"If they've got so much queer stuff out here in the barn, how much more do you suppose they've got in the house?" questioned Fred.

"If I was sure no one was at home I'd be strongly tempted to find a way inside and take a look around," said Jack.

"Come ahead and do it!" burst out Randy. "I don't believe there's a soul around."

"I'll tell you what I'll do," said Jack finally. "You keep out of sight, and I'll go out on the road and walk toward the house and knock on the door. Then, if anybody comes, I'll say that I'm out hunting and would like to buy a bit to eat. They can't refuse me a bite, and that will give me a little chance to look around while I'm inside."

"I don't think you ought to go alone," said Gif. "They know there are a bunch of us at the Lodge and they would be rather suspicious if you were by yourself. Why not let me go with you?"

So it was arranged, and, leaving the others hidden in the barn, the two cadets started to walk through the woods to the road.

"Keep your guns with you," advised Jed Wallop. "And if you git into anything like a tight place, shoot off one of the guns as a signal and we'll be to the rescue in no time."

The two boys were soon out on the lonely mountain road, and then they headed for the old house. Boldly mounting the main piazza, they knocked sharply on the door.

At first there was no response, and the lads were just congratulating themselves on the fact that the premises were deserted when they heard shuffling footsteps. Then came the tremulous voice of an elderly woman speaking in broken English.

"Who ist der? Vat you vants?"

"We are a couple of boys out hunting," answered Jack. "We would like to know if we can buy something to eat."

"I haf nodings for you. You besser go somevhere else."

"Can't we come in and get warm?" asked Gif.

"*Nein.* You go avay."

"Who lives here?" questioned Jack loudly, for the woman had made no attempt to open the door.

"Dis ist Mister Bauermann's house."

"Is he in? I'd like very much to speak to him. I am sure he would let us have something to eat," went on Jack in the smoothest tone he could command.

"Do you know Mister Bauermann?" questioned the woman cautiously.

"Isn't he the gentleman who has been riding around here in his sleigh with two or three other men?" asked Gif. "If he is," he continued, "we have met him near my father's place."

"I think you might at least let us have a little to eat. We're willing to pay well for it," broke in Jack. "Just a little bread and butter, and maybe a cup of hot coffee or tea if you have it."

"I can't open de door for you," said the woman firmly. "Mister Bauermann he gifs orders not to let anypody in de house. You haf to go avay unt get somedings to eat some-vhere else."

"When do you expect Mr. Bauermann back?" asked Gif.

"Dot I can't say. Maybe he was come back by dinner time, unt maybe not bis night."

"All right then, we'll go. But I think you are rather mean not to sell us something to eat," said Jack.

To this the woman did not make any reply, but they heard her fumbling at the door, evidently making certain that the lock and bolt were secure.

As there seemed nothing else to do, the two cadets retired, and, feeling that the woman must be watching them from behind the tightly drawn curtains at the windows, walked on down the rough road until a bend hid the house from view. Then they came up through the woods again and rejoined those at the barn.

"Well, we found out one thing, anyway," declared Jack. "There is a woman keeping guard in the house, and the menfolks are all away and won't be back until noon or to-night."

"Evidently those chaps are very secretive," said Gif. "I agree with Jack that the whole thing looks mighty suspicious."

"Do you intend to wait around here until those Germans come back?" asked Fred a bit impatiently.

"Why not go out on a hunt and come back later?" suggested Randy.

"That's the talk!" broke in Andy. "I'm getting tired of hanging around here doing nothing." To him it had been a long wait while the others had gone to the house.

"I suppose we might as well go on a hunt," announced Gif. "Anyway, I'm willing to do whatever the others say."

So it was decided that they should go off on a hunt, to return to the house either later that day or else on the day following. This suited Jed Wallop, for the old hunter did not feel in the humor for investigating the old mansion or the Germans staying there.

"Come on, come on," said he, "and maybe we'll git a chance at a fox or two."

"Now you're saying something!" cried Fred.

Leaving the old Parkingham house and outbuildings behind, they struck off through the woods, crossed the mountain road and a small frozen-up watercourse, and then mounted one of the hills lying to the northwest of Cedar Lodge. Here they found traveling rather difficult, and more than once the old hunter said he wished they were on snowshoes.

"Purty hard to use 'em at first," said he. "But after a while travelin' that way gits to be as easy as the reg'lar way."

"Oh, we know something about snowshoes," said Jack. "But we didn't think we'd need any on this trip."

They tramped around for the rest of the forenoon, managing to stir up several rabbits, and also a partridge, which Fred was fortunate enough to bring down. Then they built a small campfire and made themselves a pot of hot chocolate and had this with the lunch they had brought along.

The middle of the afternoon found them in the location Jed Wallop had had in mind when speaking of foxes. The old hunter told all of them to be on the alert.

"You know Mr. Fox ain't goin' to stand still to be shot at," said he quizzically. "As soon as he spots you he'll be off quicker than greased lightning."

They advanced with caution, and had hardly proceeded a hundred yards when Jed Wallop suddenly put up his hand for silence. They were coming to a series of rocks, and beyond this was a small clearing, backed up by brushwood still thickly covered with snow. They looked over toward this brushwood in the direction which Jed Wallop pointed out, and there saw a fox standing on a high rock, gazing expectantly at the woods beyond.

CHAPTER XXVI

WHAT THE BIG BARN CONTAINED

"There's your chance," whispered Wallop to the cadets. "Quick, now; or he may leap away before you can say Jack Robinson."

"Go ahead, Gif," said Jack quickly, for he felt that their host should have the first chance to shoot.

There was no time to argue the matter, and, raising his gun, Gif took hasty aim and fired. His aim was not of the best, for only a few of the scattering shot pierced the fox's side. The animal wheeled around in evident astonishment, and for a second did not know which way to escape.

"Fire at him! Fire at him!" called out Jed Wallop quickly. "Fire, or he'll git away."

This time all of the others blazed away, one after another. Several of the charges went wild, but Randy managed to catch the fox directly in the shoulder, and he leaped high in the air, and then came down, floundering around and kicking the loose snow in all directions.

"Hurrah! We've got him!" cried Randy.

"Mebbe you have and mebbe you haven't," answered Jed Wallop. "Better run in and finish him."

Gif was the first to do this, and a final charge caused the fox to cease his struggles.

"A purty good-sized animal," remarked the old hunter, when they were inspecting it. "That skin is worth some money."

The old hunter said he would carry the dead fox for them, and again they went forward. They spent the best part of the afternoon looking for more foxes, but in this they were disappointed. However, deep in the woods they came upon a covey of partridges. All banged away at a lively rate, and had the satisfaction of killing three of the birds.

"A pretty good haul, after all," remarked Fred, with satisfaction.

"Don't you think it about time that we returned to that old Parkingham house?" questioned Jack, after the game had been placed in their bags.

"We might as well work around that way," answered Gif. "Remember, we'll have quite a tramp after that getting back to the Lodge."

They turned in the direction of the old house in the woods and on their way kept their eyes open for more game. But all they sighted were two small squirrels, and these they thought not worth shooting at.

They were just about to cross the mountain road not far from the old house when they heard a pair of horses hitched to a long boxsled approaching. The sled was piled high with several boxes and three bales of hay.

"Get back!" cried Jack quickly. "That may be one of those Germans coming, and I don't think it would be wise to let him see us."

They stepped behind some trees and brushwood, and soon the boxsled came closer. Then another surprise awaited them, for the driver of the sled, who was alone, was none other than the farmer they had rescued from the burning railroad car.

"It's that fellow Crouse," whispered Gif. "What do you know about that?"

"Shall we go out and speak to him?" questioned Andy.

"I don't see that it would do any harm," said Jack. "We have a perfect right to be out hunting in this neighborhood."

Accordingly they stepped out in the roadway almost directly in front of the on-coming boxsled. The driver, who was crouched down with the big collar of his overcoat turned up around his ears, had evidently been in deep thought, for when he noticed them he straightened up in surprise and brought his team to a sudden halt.

"Why, if it isn't our friend from the railroad train!" remarked Jack, with a smile.

"Well, I never!" declared Herman Crouse, with a momentary look of pleasure on his face. "How did you young gentlemen get up here?" And then, of a sudden, a cloud came over his features.

"Can't you see we're out hunting?" answered Fred, pointing to the guns and game in their bags.

"Yes, yes! To be sure! I forgot that you came up here to go hunting. Have you had much success?"

"A little," answered Gif. "We've got a fox, and we've had quite a few rabbits, squirrels, quail and partridges."

"Not so bad." Herman Crouse looked anxiously at the boys and Jed Wallop. "Where are you staying?"

"At Cedar Lodge. It's several miles from here," answered Jack. And then he continued: "You belong around here? I thought you said you had a farm near Enwood."

"So I have. But during the winter I make a little extra money trucking. That's what I am doing now. I am feeling pretty good again."

"Where are you bound?" questioned Randy.

At this question Herman Crouse seemed somewhat disturbed.

"Oh, I've got to go up the road quite a distance," he answered evasively. "I might offer to give you a ride, only you can see I am loaded down as it is." And this statement was correct, for the boxsled was carrying about all the team could haul.

"We met some other Germans around here—four men who drive around in a big sleigh," said Jack boldly and looking Herman Crouse full in the eyes.

"Yes, yes! I know!" The eyes of the man fell for an instant. "I am not a German," he said somewhat lamely. "That is, I was born on the other side, but I came to this country before I was twenty-one, and now I am an American."

"Then you don't side with Germany in this war?"

"I don't side with the Kaiser. I am sorry for the common people, for they have had no say-so in this awful slaughter that is going on."

"Well, I'm glad to hear that you stick up for the good old U. S. A.!" cried Jack. "You know there are a good many Germans and German-Americans here who are the other way."

"I want nothing to do with them and nothing to do with war!" answered Herman Crouse. "I am only a hard-working man who wants to be left alone." He paused for an instant. "Don't imagine that I have forgotten what you did for me," he continued, with a little smile. "You were my very good friends, and I shall never forget it. Now, if you please, I must hurry on, because I want to get back home before it gets too dark. I wish you all the best of luck with your hunting;" and he took up the reins again.

"Do you know anything about the hunting in that direction?" questioned Randy, pointing to where the old Parkingham house was located.

"I do not think it is very good up there," was the quick reply. "And, anyway, if I were you gentlemen I would not go anywhere near the old house up there."

"Why not?" demanded Jed Wallop.

"The people who are staying there are very queer. They do not like any strangers around."

"Then you know them?" questioned Gif.

"Yes, I know them, but not very well. Some of them are German-Americans, like me, but they are not my friends. I would advise you to stay away from them. The hunting, anyway, is better elsewhere. Now good-bye and good luck." And thus speaking, Herman Crouse urged forward his team and continued on his way.

"I'll bet a new hat against a lemon that he is bound for the old Parkingham house!" exclaimed Randy, when the German was out of earshot.

"Let us follow him and make sure," returned his twin.

"All right," said Jack. "But we had better keep out of sight among the trees."

With so much timber standing around, this was an easy matter. Following Crouse, they saw the man at last turn in at the old house and drive around to where the barn was located. Then he got out of the boxsled and walked to a back door of the residence.

"Now I guess we'll find out if those Germans are back or not," announced Gif.

They waited for several minutes, and then the door was again opened and Herman Crouse came out, followed by two of the men the boys had previously seen. All three hurried down to the barn and there began to unload the boxsled. Then the boys saw the unknown Germans give Crouse some money. The three talked together for a few minutes in German, and then the owner of the boxsled drove away and the other Germans returned to the house.

"This is getting interesting," remarked Jack. "Of course, that hay was meant for the horses, but what do you suppose can be in those packing cases?"

"Come on around to the back of the barn, and maybe we can learn something further," said Fred.

"It's gettin' purty late, boys," announced Jed Wallop.

"If you want to go home, don't let us keep you," returned Gif, quickly.

"Well, I don't want to see any of you lads git into trouble," answered Wallop. "At the same time, I hate to leave my family alone after dark."

"Well, you go on, then," put in Jack quickly. "There are five of us, and I guess we can take care of ourselves, especially as we have our guns with us."

"O' course, everything may be perfectly reg'lar here," continued Jed Wallop. "Although, like you, I have my doubts. But unless you want me to stay, I'll git home." And a little later he took his departure.

Left to themselves, the Rovers and Gif watched their chance, and, unobserved, entered the big barn. Here they found that all of the packing cases which had been brought in by Herman Crouse had been placed out of sight under the hay.

"One thing is certain—they don't want any outsiders to know about these cases," remarked Jack.

Suddenly Fred, who was looking out of the doorway toward the house, uttered a low cry of alarm.

"Get under cover, fellows, just as quick as you can!" he said. "Three of those Germans are coming down here!"

CHAPTER XXVII

THE COMING OF THE WOLVES

Fred's announcement came as a surprise. The Germans were coming from the house so rapidly that there was no time to leave the barn, the back door being closed and having some packing cases and hay against it.

"Come on up in the loft!" cried Jack. "Be quick now!"

"Why not hide down here in the hay?" suggested Andy.

"Because they may try to get at those packing cases, and then they would probably discover us," was the reply. "Quick! This way!"

Gif was already acting on the oldest Rover boy's suggestion and going up a ladder nailed to one side of the barn. Randy and the others followed, Fred being the last.

At the top of the ladder was an opening to a large loft. Here there was more hay, and also some old farm implements which had evidently been hoisted there by means of a block and tackle.

"Hush now," warned Gif, and the five cadets tiptoed their

way toward the hay, bent upon secreting themselves should it become necessary to do so.

The Germans carried two lanterns, for it was now quite dark in the barn. They were talking volubly in their native tongue, so that the cadets could understand very little of what was said. One man, a tall, burly individual, who was evidently more prosperous than the others, was addressed as Herr Bauermann, and he was the man mentioned by the woman who had refused to open the door and let Jack and Gif in.

Herr Bauermann had come out to inspect the contents of the packing cases brought in by Herman Crouse. He had the two other men open the cases and take out layers of excelsior so that he might look at what was underneath. He gave a grunt of satisfaction and nodded his head approvingly, at the same time continuing to speak in German.

All of the cadets were anxious to see what the boxes contained, and looked cautiously down the ladder opening and through some cracks in the loft flooring. All they could make out was some machinery, apparently electrical and similar to that in the other cases. There was also a large round package covered with heavy bagging, and this was found to contain more coils of wire of various sizes.

While the men were looking around one of them suddenly stooped and picked up something from the floor. He passed this to the others, at the same time making some remark which, of course, the lads could not understand.

"He's got a glove," whispered Jack.

"It's one of my gloves! I dropped it when we climbed the ladder," returned Randy in sudden alarm.

Arthur M. Winfield

The finding of the glove interested the Germans very much. They looked all around the barn, and for a few minutes the cadets were fearful that they would come up in the loft. But then they evidently concluded that the glove had been dropped by Herman Crouse, and placed it on a shelf.

It was a good half hour before the Germans left the barn and returned to the house, and by that time the five cadets in the loft were almost frozen. They had been unable to move around and thus keep warm, and with the coming of night the thermometer was going down steadily.

"Come on! let us get out of here," said Fred, his teeth chattering. "If we don't move soon I'll be frozen stiff."

The boys came cautiously out of the barn and looked toward the house. Every curtain was tightly drawn, and lights shown only from the kitchen and the dining room of the old dwelling.

"Those fellows are going to get supper," said Randy, "and I move we go home and do likewise. We can't learn anything more standing here, and if we went to the door and showed ourselves those men might get very suspicious."

"All right! let's go back to the Lodge then," announced Jack. "Just the same, I'm going to investigate this matter further, and I'm not going to wait so very long either."

"Oh, I guess we all want to investigate these Germans," said Fred quickly. "Don't you remember how we helped to round up those submarine rascals?" he added, referring to an affair which has been related in detail in the volume entitled, "The Rover Boys Under Canvas."

Losing no more time, the five cadets hurried down the rough

mountain road, and then struck off through the woods on a bee line for Cedar Lodge. This time Gif took good care that they should not become lost. But it was a long wearisome journey, and before the Lodge was reached every one of the lads was almost ready to drop from exhaustion. They were bitterly cold, and some of them thought their ears or noses must be frozen.

"There's the light!" cried Fred at last, and he pointed to a candle which Spouter had had Stowell place in one of the windows.

"Spouter must have done that to help us to find the way," said Jack. "Very thoughtful of him."

As soon as they were a little closer they set up a ringing shout, and at once Henry Stowell came to the door and flung it open. All were glad enough to troop in and throw themselves down in comfortable seats before the blazing fire.

"Me for a big hot supper!" announced Randy. "And I can't get it inside of me any too quick!"

"Ditto right here," added Fred.

"And don't forget to pass me a large portion, please," came from Andy.

Under Spouter's directions, Stowell had already set a pot of water to boiling, and had likewise baked a large pan of pork and beans and made another pan of biscuits. Even though he had asked the sneak of Colby Hall to work, Spouter had spoken kindly to Stowell and given him some first-class advice, and this was evidently having its effect.

"I've got my skates, and I'm going to skate down to Henryville to-morrow," said Stowell. "From there I can take the public sleigh to Timminsport, and go home that way. Wish I was there now!"

Soon supper was under way, and, while eating, the other cadets related to their chum what they had seen and heard around the old house in the woods.

"There sure is something wrong up there," declared Spouter, whose sprained ankle was much better. "Those fellows are up to no good. I think, Jack, we ought to notify the authorities."

"We talked that over, Spouter; and we have concluded that we will take another look around the place first," was the reply.

The others questioned Stowell again, but could get little further information from the young cadet. He was satisfied, however, that Werner had been doing some queer things for Tony Duval, and that Bill Glutts had assisted his crony.

"There is something strange about the whole business," said he. "Once or twice I asked Bill or Gabe about it, but I never could get any satisfaction. I sometimes think carrying that message was only a bluff, and that the Germans were merely trying to test out Bill and Gabe, to see if they could not get them to do something else."

In the morning came a big surprise. It was snowing and blowing furiously, and to go hunting or to do anything else outside was practically out of the question. The windows were coated with ice.

"I guess I'll have to stay with you fellows for awhile," remarked Stowell dolefully. "I wouldn't dare to try to get to

Henryville in such a snowstorm as this."

"You stay right where you are, Henry, and make yourself comfortable," said Gif. "As long as you're willing to do your share of the work around here, you shall have your share of whatever there is to eat."

"It's very nice of you fellows to treat me this way after all that has happened," said the young cadet. "Of course I'll do my full share of the work. When I was with Bill and Gabe they always wanted me to do everything."

The storm continued all that day, the wind, if anything, increasing in violence. All the boys could do was to keep the fire going and make themselves as comfortable as possible inside the Lodge. They read, wrote letters, and played games, and also tried their hands at more candy-making, and also the baking of some pies and cookies.

"Gee! those pies are pretty good," announced Spouter, after a piece of one of them had been passed to him.

"They ought to be good," returned Fred. "My face was nearly burned off baking them."

"And please don't ask me to make any more doughnuts," announced Randy. "If I had to run a bake shop, I'd charge about twice as much as the regular bakers do."

"He'd charge for the hole in the doughnut," came from his twin, with a grin.

During the day they had once or twice heard a sound outside that was new to them. They were not sure, but Jack thought it might be a wolf, and to this Gif agreed.

236   Arthur M. Winfield

"There are wolves prowling around here," said the latter. "But I never knew of any to come close to the Lodge."

"More than likely he's hungry and wants something to eat, and has smelled our stuff cooking," ventured Fred.

They had an early supper, and then Gif said they would have to get in another supply of wood from the shed before retiring.

"And we might as well get in a good supply while we are at it," he added. "If this snow keeps coming down we may not be able to get out at all to-morrow unless we do a lot of shoveling."

It was no easy job to get to the woodshed, for the wind was still blowing furiously. When they opened the back door of the Lodge the snow came swirling in, almost blinding them.

"No use of you fellows trying it," announced Jack to Fred and Stowell.

"That's it," said Gif. "Four of us going out will be more than enough. You fellows can push the snow away from the door if you want to."

With their overcoats buttoned up tightly and their caps pulled well down over their ears, Gif, Jack and the twins sallied forth in the direction of the woodshed, which was about fifty yards away. They had all they could do to make any progress, and when the shed was gained they were almost winded.

"Say, we were foolish not to get this wood before," panted Gif.

"Well, there is no use of finding fault now," answered Jack. "Come on. Now we have packed down the path a little it won't be quite so hard."

The four boys made two trips to the woodshed, each time bringing all the logs they could carry. Then Randy wanted to call a halt.

"I'm about played out," said he. "Let us get the rest in to-morrow."

"That's just what I say," gasped his twin. "No use of killing ourselves."

"I'm going to make one more trip," said Gif.

"And so am I," added Jack.

The pair stepped out of the house with the others watching them. In a minute more they disappeared from view in the storm and the darkness.

"Gee! but it's going to be one awful night," cried Fred.

"You've said it!" returned Randy. Then, of a sudden, he gave a start. "What's that?" he ejaculated.

What he referred to was a long mournful howl which arose on the storm-laden air. This howl was followed by another, and then by a third.

"It's wolves!" cried Fred.

"Look! Look!" ejaculated Andy. "Look out there, will you? A whole pack of wolves!"

Arthur M. Winfield

"Yes, and they're coming right for the house!" wailed Stowell. "Shut that door quick, or they'll jump in on us!"

CHAPTER XXVIII

THE MAN IN THE GREY OVERCOAT

"Don't shut the door!" cried Randy. "Remember, Gif and Jack are outside."

"Hello out there!" yelled Spouter, hobbling to the door in the excitement. "Beware of the wolves!"

Whether his voice carried to Jack and Gif through the storm they could not tell. Then came another howl from the wolves, this time in concert, and suddenly two of the slinking forms appeared close to the open door. The eyes of the beasts appeared so baneful to the cadets that they quickly slammed the barrier shut and bolted it.

"But we can't leave Jack and Gif out there!" cried Fred. "Remember! they are unarmed."

"Get the guns!" ordered Spouter. "Hurry up! We'll give those wolves all they are looking for."

He hobbled across the floor to his own weapon, resting against the wall in a corner, and looked to see if it was loaded. The others also made a wild dash to arm themselves.

Arthur M. Winfield

In the meanwhile the howls of the wolves kept increasing. Two more of the beasts had come up close to the Lodge, so that the total number was now five.

"Oh, oh! do you think they'll break into the house and eat us up?" wailed Stowell.

"If they break in they'll get one mighty warm reception," answered Andy. "Come on! let us open that door and go after them," he continued boldly.

Now that they were armed the Rovers and Spouter felt much safer, and they lost no time in getting back to the door which they had just closed.

"Oh, dear! don't open the door," pleaded Stowell. "They'll jump right in on top of us!"

"Not after we give 'em a few doses of shot," answered Spouter. "Here, Henry, you stand behind the door along with Fred. You, Andy and Randy, fire as soon as you catch sight of the wolves. I'll reserve my shot for any beast that tries to enter."

"Wait!" called out Randy suddenly. "When you shoot at the wolves be sure to aim low. Otherwise the shots may carry through the storm and hit Gif or Jack."

The door was opened cautiously by Fred, Stowell being too frightened to assist. Those ready to fire saw several of the wolves in a bunch less than fifteen feet away. The beasts had found some scraps of food which had been thrown out of the bungalow and were pawing for more in the snow.

"Bang! bang!" went the shotguns in the hands of the twins. The wolves gave loud yelps of pain, and one leaped high in the air. Another uttered a fierce snarl, and then, seeing the young hunters, made a dash directly for them.

It was a moment of great peril, for the wolf had been wounded just enough to make it tremendously ugly. Its eyes gleamed wickedly, and it showed every tooth in its wide-open mouth.

But Spouter was on guard. He waited until the wolf was less than five feet from the door, and then blazed away. The charge of shot was so heavy that the beast fell back, its neck completely shattered.

"Now give 'em a second barrel, boys!" cried Spouter, and a moment later three more reports rang out.

Then, unable to resist the temptation to get into the fight, Fred caught up his gun and also fired, managing to catch one of the fleeing beasts in the hind quarters.

"I guess that's the last of those wolves," remarked Spouter. "I don't believe they'll come around here again all winter."

The wolf shot through the neck was dead, while at least two of the others were so badly wounded they could scarcely drag themselves away through the storm. The others disappeared as if by magic, racing along at the top of their speed.

"Hello there!" came from out of the storm. "How did you make out with those wolves?" It was Jack who was calling, and a moment later he appeared with Gif following.

"There is what is left of the pack!" cried Randy, pointing to the dead wolf. "Spouter brought that one down, and we managed to wound at least two others."

"And those that could do it left quicker than them came," added his twin.

"Good for you, Spouter!" cried Jack. "Evidently spraining your ankle didn't interfere with your marksmanship."

"Huh! anybody could hit a target if he was right on top of it," answered the other cadet; nevertheless Spouter was immensely pleased over his success in laying the big wolf low.

The carcass of the dead beast was dragged into the entryway, and then Gif and Jack brought a few more sticks of wood from the shed.

"We'll have to skin that wolf," said Gif. "Spouter, you can get a very nice rug out of it, or maybe use the fur for some kind of a garment."

"I'll send it home," said Spouter. "I know it will please the folks very much."

It was not until some days later that the storm cleared away sufficiently for the boys to go out once more. Then, as they were running short of supplies, they decided to accompany Stowell down to Henryville, going as before on their skates.

"I must say I rather hate to leave you fellows," declared the little cadet. "You've treated me very nicely—much better than I was treated by Bill and Gabe. When we get back to Colby Hall I won't forget it."

"Well, you turn over a new leaf, Henry, and join the right crowd, and you'll get along much better," answered Jack. "It will never do a fellow any good to train with chaps like Glutts and Werner or with fellows like Nappy Martell and

Slugger Brown."

They found quite a little snow on the river and had often to plough across the drifts on their skates as best they could. But there were many long, cleared spaces, and here all of the cadets made good time, for even Stowell was a fairly good skater.

"You'll be just in time, Henry," said Gif, as they came in sight of the town. "It's now half-past ten, and, if I remember rightly, the public sleigh for Timminsport leaves at eleven o'clock."

Gif's surmise proved correct and all walked over to the hotel from which the sleigh for the other town started. It was an easy matter for Stowell to obtain accommodations in this turnout, and soon he had said good-bye and was bound for home.

"I'm mighty glad he is going to give up training with Glutts and Werner," remarked Fred, and the others agreed with him.

The boys had made out a list of what they wanted, and, leaving the hotel, they went over to the general store where they had traded before. The proprietor was glad to see them, especially when he found out they needed so many things.

"I had a man in here last night asking about you," said the storekeeper when he was busy putting up their things.

"Asking about us?" repeated Jack. "Who was he?"

"I don't know. He was in here once before, two or three weeks ago asking about the different hunting lodges and lumber camps in this vicinity. He didn't give any name, and he didn't say what his business was."

"What sort of looking man was he?" asked Gif.

"Oh, just an ordinary looking sort of fellow—not very tall and not very short either. He had a clean-shaven face and dark hair and dark eyes."

"How was he dressed?" questioned Fred.

"He wore a dark grey overcoat and a slouch hat and fur gloves. He bought a couple of my best cigars, and stood around awhile, talking about the people who came to the store to trade. Then he asked about Cedar Lodge, and he wanted to know all about who was staying there. When he heard the name Rover he was very much interested, and when I told him you were a bunch of cadets from Colby Hall he said he would have to look you up."

"Maybe he's a friend of ours!" cried Randy. "Too bad you didn't get the name."

"I don't know as he was any particular friend. You see, he asked about some of the other places around here too—about Jed Wallop's place, and those shacks belonging to Tony Duval, and about the old Hunker cabin and the deserted Parkingham house, and the old Crosby camp, and those shacks down at Miller's saw mill, and a lot of places like that. I thought maybe he had an idea of buying some place and locating here."

"He may have been nothing but a real estate agent," declared Andy.

"What did you tell him about the old Parkingham house?" questioned Jack curiously.

"I told him a bunch of foreigners were staying up there—I

thought possibly they might be Germans trying to hide themselves so as to keep out of the draft. Say! do you suppose he might be a Government agent rounding up the slackers?" continued the storekeeper, with interest.

"I'm sure I don't know," answered Jack. "If he calls again ask him his name, and if he is a friend of ours tell him we would be glad to see him up at the lodge at any time."

"All right, I'll do that."

Had they not been hampered by so many bundles and packages, some of which were quite heavy, the cadets would have remained out hunting for the rest of the day. But as it was, they decided to skate directly home and obtain a belated lunch at the Lodge, and then, if they felt like it, go out later.

"We're up here just for the fun of it, so there is no necessity of being too strenuous," said Gif. "We want to go back to Colby Hall feeling really refreshed."

They had reached the river once more, and were busy putting on their skates, when they heard a shout behind them. Turning, they beheld a man who, as soon as he saw they were looking in his direction, waved his hand at them.

"Excuse me, but are some of you the Rover boys?" he questioned, as he came closer.

"Yes," answered Jack. "I am one of the Rovers, and these are my cousins," and he indicated the others.

"I was up at the store, and the storekeeper told me you had just gone away and were bound up the river. If you don't mind, I would like to have a talk with you."

Arthur M. Winfield

The man was of medium size, with dark hair and dark eyes, and as he wore a dark grey overcoat and a slouch hat, the cadets immediately put him down for the individual mentioned to them by the storekeeper. He had a quiet smile on his face which was reassuring to all of the lads.

"What is it you want to know?" questioned Fred.

"Are you the Rovers from Colby Hall—the young men who had so much to do with rounding up those Germans at Camp Barlight and capturing that hidden submarine?"

"Yes."

"And you also helped in rounding up those other fellows who were trying to put through some deal with two men named Brown and Martell?"

"We did," said Andy.

"It was a fine thing to do, and it shows that you fellows are true blue," returned the man, with satisfaction.

"Are you a Secret Service man?" questioned Jack suddenly.

"Why do you want to know that, Rover?" was the counter question.

"If you belong to the Secret Service you are just the man we are looking for."

CHAPTER XXIX

WHAT HAPPENED AT THE LODGE

"So you want to see a Secret Service man, eh?" said the newcomer, after a slight pause. "What's in the wind?"

"We think we have discovered something that the Government ought to know about," answered Jack slowly.

"But there isn't any use of our saying anything about it unless you are really a public official of some sort or other," broke in Randy hastily.

After this there followed quite a conversation, the newcomer leading the boys on to tell what they knew concerning the Germans at the old Parkingham house, and also what they knew about Herman Crouse and Tony Duval.

"I think I am on the right track at last," said the man. "And since you have told me so much I will return your confidences by stating that I *am* a Secret Service officer. We had an idea that the Germans might try something of that sort in this vicinity, and I am pretty sure now that we are on the right track."

"Try something of what sort?" questioned Andy.

"We received word in a roundabout way over six weeks ago that an attempt would be made by the Germans to establish a radio station somewhere along this portion of the coast. The hills back of Timminsport and Henryville would make an ideal spot for such a station."

"Do you mean a radio station from which they could send wireless messages all the way to Germany?" cried Fred.

"Oh, no! Not such a distance as that. Such a station would require more power than they would be able to generate without heavy and complicated machinery. But it was thought they might establish a lesser station from which they could send wireless messages to any of their submarines or warships that might be sailing within a given distance of our shore."

"You surely have struck it!" cried Randy. "Those coils of wire and the electrical things we saw in the packing cases up at their barn prove it."

The Secret Service agent, who gave his name as William Pollock, questioned them still further, and then said he would get into immediate communication with his superiors.

"You'll hear more from me in the near future," said he, when the talk had come to an end. "I'll probably be at Cedar Lodge in two or three days. In the meantime, if you want to do Uncle Sam a real service say nothing at all to any outsider of what you have discovered, or of your meeting with me."

To this the cadets readily consented, and then William Pollock hurried off, to obtain a private turnout in which to get to Timminsport as speedily as possible.

"Now I guess there will be something doing up at the

Parkingham house before long," declared Gif, when they were once more on their way to the Lodge.

"Yes, and there will be something doing at Tony Duval's place too," returned Jack.

"I wish we could be on hand to see what happens!" cried Randy wistfully.

"Perhaps, if the Secret Service men come up here to make an arrest, they will allow us to go along with them," added his twin.

On account of his ankle, which was still somewhat weak, Spouter had remained at the bungalow. When the others returned he listened with keen interest to all they had to tell.

"Gee, that's great!" he exclaimed. "If those Germans are really guilty I hope the government officials round them up in short order."

"Yes, and round up Tony Duval, too," added Fred.

"What about Glutts and Werner?" questioned Andy.

"Well, if they have been guilty of any treachery toward our Government, they ought to suffer," was the way Gif expressed himself.

"Do you know, I'll feel rather sorry for that Herman Crouse, if he is mixed up in this," said Jack. "He seemed to be a pretty decent sort."

"Well, in these war times a man has either got to be for Uncle Sam or against him," answered Spouter.

Feeling certain that William Pollock would be unable to do anything that afternoon, the boys got a hasty lunch, and late in the afternoon went out for some more hunting. They tramped a distance of over two miles through the snow, and managed to bring down several rabbits and likewise a pheasant and some smaller birds.

"I hope we don't see any more of those wolves," said Fred, when they had started to return to the Lodge.

"Look! look!" cried Gif suddenly.

He had scarcely spoken when Jack raised his gun and fired. Then the oldest Rover boy fired again, both shots being taken before the others could get their guns into action.

"It's a fox!" cried Randy. "Jack, I guess you got him, too!"

"I hope so," was Jack's answer as he stopped to reload his weapon.

The animal he had fired at had been running across a small opening between the trees. At the first shot the game had made a turn, and at the second had given a leap and disappeared into a small hollow filled with snow.

When the boys reached the hollow all they could see at first was the snow which had been kicked in several directions. But then they caught sight of a bushy tail peeping forth from the white covering.

"It's a fox, all right enough!" exclaimed Gif.

"Look out there! He may not be dead," warned Fred. "If he's alive and you touch him he may give you quite a bite."

They advanced with caution, and Gif turned the animal over with the end of his gun barrel. He exposed a large fox of a silvery grey color. It was quite dead.

"A silver fox!" came from Andy.

"Jack, you've had your wish," said Gif. "It's a silver fox, all right enough."

They dragged it forth from the hollow and examined the animal with much interest. The fur was somewhat reddish next to the hide, but the tips were white and silver grey.

"A beautiful piece of fur, that's certain," said Gif. "Your folks will be glad to get it."

"How about Ruth Stevenson getting it," said Randy, with a grin; and at this remark Jack blushed.

A part of the next day was spent in skinning both the fox and the wolf. The boys wondered if they would see anything of the Secret Service agent, but he did not show himself.

"They may take their own time about working up this case," remarked Spouter. "They may want to get just the right kind of evidence before they close in on the rascals."

Another day went by, and again the lads went forth to try their skill both at hunting and at fishing. This time Spouter went along, and while the others were fishing with more or less success the orator of Colby Hall had the honor of stirring up a brook mink of fair size and laying it low.

"You've got a nice little neck-piece there for somebody," said Jack, as he looked at the soft fur of the mink. "You can count yourself lucky."

Arthur M. Winfield

Another Sunday was passed in camp, but still the Secret Service agent did not show himself. On the Sabbath day Jed Wallop came down to see them. They said nothing to the old hunter of what was in the wind.

"I am sorry to hear your vacation is drawin' to a close," said Jed Wallop. "But you ought to be purty well satisfied over what you've got. It ain't everybody that can git a silver fox and other foxes too, and a wolf and a brook mink, not to say anything about rabbits, squirrels, partridges, and sech. I think you lads have done wonderful well."

"I think so myself," answered Gif.

Monday morning the young hunters took it easy, and it was not until after lunch that they thought of going out once again with their guns.

"Might as well make the best of what time is left to us," was the way Fred expressed himself. "Before long we'll have to be at the Colby Hall grind again."

"Don't mention school to me," answered Andy. "This kind of a life suits me down to the heels."

The boys were almost ready to leave the Lodge when they heard the jingle of sleigh bells and to their surprise saw a large sled approaching filled with the bundled-up figures of men.

"Hello, it must be those Secret Service agents!" cried Gif. "Now maybe there will be something doing!"

All watched the approach of the big sleigh, and were then surprised to see that the turnout contained the four Germans they had met before, and likewise Tony Duval and a sixth man, who was a stranger to them.

"Are you at home?" called out the largest of the Germans, the man named Bauermann.

"Looks as if we were, doesn't it?" answered Jack, as he stood in the doorway with the others peering over his shoulders.

"We would like to have a talk with you, young man," went on Emil Bauermann, with a frown on his face. "We came over here on purpose to see you."

"If you young men have been trying to make trouble for me you shall suffer for it," came in a growl from Tony Duval.

"Who said we were trying to make trouble for you, Duval?" demanded Gif.

"Bah! you cannot fool me, Garrison," said the hunter wrathfully. Evidently he was greatly excited.

"Duval, let me handle this matter," remonstrated Emil Bauermann. "We want to have a serious talk with you young men," he added to the boys.

All of the occupants of the big sleigh sprang out in the snow, and without waiting for an invitation to do so stalked into the Lodge.

The Germans were evidently in a bad humor, and they glowered at the cadets in a way that made them feel far from comfortable.

"What is it you want?" demanded Gif, not liking the manner of their intrusion.

"We want to come to an understanding," growled one of the Germans.

"You cannot play tricks behind our backs without taking the consequences," grumbled another.

"Maybe you think you're smart, but you'll find that we are smarter," added a third. "Many a man has been so smart that he has stuck his head into the noose."

"Let me handle this matter," broke in Emil Bauermann, and then uttered some words in German. An animated discussion in that tongue followed, the cadets understanding next to nothing of what was said.

"I do not like the looks of this at all," whispered Randy to Jack. "I believe they came here to do us harm."

"That's the way it looks to me too," whispered Fred. "They must have got wind in some way of our being up around their place."

The Germans had turned to the strange man who was with them, and when they pointed to the cadets this stranger nodded. Evidently he was identifying the boys.

"It is as I thought," said Emil Bauermann sternly, as he glared at the young hunters. "This man saw you spying around our place and around the Duval place. What do you mean by such conduct? Explain yourselves or take my word for it, it will go hard with you," and he shook a menacing fist in their faces.

CHAPTER XXX

THE EXPOSURE—CONCLUSION

It must be confessed that the six cadets did not like the menacing attitude of the five Germans and Tony Duval. Evidently one of the men—the stranger—had been spying on them, and he had carried his information to the others.

"That's right, Bauermann, make them explain themselves," growled Tony Duval. "And don't be too easy on 'em, either!"

"See here, you have no right to come in here without being invited," said Gif angrily.

"Poof! what are you but a pack of silly schoolboys?" growled the German. "Perhaps you thought you were doing a wonderful thing spying around our house and our barn? You didn't know we had someone watching you all the time."

"Yes, and watching you also when you spied on Duval," broke in another of the men.

"Well, what do you want?" questioned Randy, after a brief and ominous pause.

"We want you to tell us just what you have discovered and

Arthur M. Winfield

what you propose to do about it," answered Emil Bauermann. "And remember, I want the plain truth! No beating about the bush!" and he shook a warning finger at the cadets.

While the man was speaking Jack had stepped to the rear of the crowd. Now he made a movement to pick up his gun, but at this one of the Germans rushed forward, pulling a pistol from his pocket as he did so.

"Stop that! Don't you dare to touch that gun!" the man roared threateningly.

"You can't order us around in our own house," declared Gif. "If you are going to talk like that you can get out."

"We'll stay as long as we please; and if you boys don't behave yourselves, so much the worse for you," answered Emil Bauermann. "We are going to get to the bottom of your tricks, and do it now."

"Suppose we have nothing to say," said Andy.

"But you will say something," stormed another of the Germans. "If you don't—well, you will take the conesquences, that's all."

After this the Germans did their best to make the cadets give all the particulars regarding their visit to Tony Duval's shack, and also to the house and barn on the Parkingham place. They were anxious to ascertain just how much the boys knew, and also how much they suspected.

But the cadets were on their guard, and refused to answer many of the questions put to them. This infuriated both the Germans and Duval, and for the time being it looked as if a fight was coming and the cadets might get the worst of it. All of the men were armed, and they did not permit any of the young hunters to touch their weapons. Instead, one of the men was ordered by Bauermann to confiscate the guns. And this he did, placing them in a heap outside of the Lodge.

Seeing they could get very little out of the cadets, and suspecting that the lads were getting ready to notify the authorities, the Germans held another consultation in their own tongue and then called Duval to one side.

"Just as I expected, we'll have to make prisoners of them for the time being," said Emil Bauermann to Duval. "We can take them up in the mountains, to that log cabin you spoke about."

"But we can't take them in the sleigh," answered Duval.

"Then you and two of my men will have to march them up there on foot. We can come up later and bring you supplies."

"Do you think it's as bad as all that?" questioned Tony Duval nervously.

"I do! They have learned too much! And if word of this got to the authorities it might go hard with all of us."

Thereupon the six cadets were ordered to get their belongings together and prepare to leave the Lodge. All demurred, but the Germans and Duval showed their weapons and acted so threateningly that there was nothing left to do but to obey.

"This is the worst yet!" groaned Fred. "Where in the world do they intend to take us?"

"Don't ask me," replied Randy dismally.

"If only we could get at our guns," whispered Gif.

"Let's make a dash for them," suggested Jack.

"Yes, and get shot down on the spot!" returned Spouter.

With their belongings over their shoulders, the six cadets had just been marched out of the Lodge when there came an unexpected interruption. Glancing toward the river, Jack saw a body of men approaching. They were at least eight or ten in number, and the man in the lead was William Pollock.

"Look! look!" whispered the oldest Rover boy to the others. "There is that Secret Service agent, and he has an armed posse with him."

"Grab the guns and make for the Lodge," suggested Randy.

A shout came from the woods as Pollock approached. This surprised the Germans and Duval, and, noting the number of men coming on, they were bewildered and did not know what to do. It was just such a diversion as the boys were hoping for, and in a trice they had rushed for their guns and secured their weapons. Then Jack sent up a shout.

"Mr. Pollock! Mr. Pollock! This way! Here are those Germans now! And Tony Duval is with them!"

The things that happened next came so rapidly that it is almost impossible to describe them. At first the Germans and Duval sought to make resistance, and several shots were fired by them. The boys and some of the Secret Service posse fired in return, and Duval was struck in the arm and one of the Germans got a bullet through his leg. Then the

Germans and Duval made a rush for the sleigh in an endeavor to escape.

But William Pollock and his men had handled such desperate characters before. Two of them leaped in front of the moving horses and stopped them, while the others surrounded the men in the sleigh and pointed their guns at the fellows.

"Hands up, all of you!" ordered Pollock sternly. "Quick now, if you don't want us to fire!"

At heart the Germans were cowards, and even though they still held their pistols, when they saw the uplifted guns of, not alone the posse, but also the cadets, pointed at them, they raised their hands without further protest, and Tony Duval did the same; and thus the brief but sharp encounter came to a termination.

"You are making a terrible mistake," said Emil Bauermann lamely. "We have done no wrong."

"You can tell your story in court," answered William Pollock briefly, and thereafter he made the Germans and Duval give up all their weapons. Then he had some of his men search the evildoers and take from them whatever papers and documents they carried. When he had a list of their names he looked well satisfied.

"Bauermann, we have been trying to round you up for the past six months," said he sternly. "You know you are wanted for that little affair in Philadelphia." And at this the German looked much disturbed.

The cadets were exceedingly thankful for the opportune arrival of the Secret Service man and his posse.

Arthur M. Winfield

"Well, I told you I would come," said he. "I was delayed a little though. You know in these war times matters do not always move as swiftly as one would want. A good deal of the credit for this haul goes to you boys," he added with a smile.

Much to the surprise of the cadets, in the crowd of new-comers was Herman Crouse. The German-American farmer seemed well satisfied with what had taken place.

"Mr. Pollock knows that I am true-blue," said he. "That Bauermann and the rest of his gang thought they could use me. But I have fooled them nicely. There is but one country for old Herman Crouse, and that is the good old United States of America," and his face beamed as he spoke.

"That's the right way to talk!" cried Jack. "You don't know how pleased I am to know the man we hauled out of that train wreck is true-blue."

"If we had thought you were a traitorous German, we might have left you to shift for yourself," added Randy. "Although maybe I wouldn't have had the heart to do that, either," he added, on second thought.

After the Germans and Duval had been made prisoners they were left at the Lodge in charge of two of the Secret Service men and the cadets. Then William Pollock and the other men took the sleigh and lost no time in making their way to the old Parkingham house. They had some trouble with the old German housekeeper, but wasted no words with her and finally compelled her to tell all she knew. The old house was ransacked from top to bottom for evidence against the Germans, after which the posse turned its attention to the contents of the barn.

The results were as William Pollock had anticipated. These Germans, aided by a number of others and also by Duval, were getting ready to erect a fair-sized radio station in the woods behind the old house. Duval had carried many messages for them and also done some trucking. He was hand-in-glove with them, willing to make money at any cost. He told later that both his mother and his grand-mother had been Germans.

As Herman Crouse had said, he had been used to do some trucking for the Germans, and had likewise been asked to perform a number of errands. But gradually he had become suspicious of the men, and was thinking seriously of notifying the authorities when the cadets appeared on the scene.

"And what about Bill Glutts and Gabe Werner?" questioned Jack of William Pollock later on, when the Secret Service men were getting ready to take the Germans and Duval away.

"I can't tell you all the particulars about those two young fellows," answered the Secret Service man. "The Germans evidently used them, but whether Glutts and Werner knew the truth of what the Germans were doing remains to be found out."

It may be added here that Glutts and Werner were very much scared over the position in which they found themselves, and when the Germans and Duval came up for a hearing the parents of the two young fellows had all they could do to convince the authorities that Gabe and Bill were really patriotic.

"Well, I'm mighty glad we are clear of those Germans, and of Tony Duval, too," said Gif, after the evildoers had been taken away. "Now maybe we can finish our outing in peace."

And this they did. Jed Wallop came over to see them and went out with the young hunters a number of times. No larger game appeared, but they brought down a number of rabbits and squirrels, as well as partridges and some smaller birds, and with this they had to be content.

During those days the boys received several letters from the girls, and also a letter from Mrs. Tom Rover enclosing one from her husband in France. This latter epistle stated that the writer and his brother Sam had recovered from the shell wounds received, and that Dick Rover was no longer suffering from the effects of the gas attack he had experienced.

"Gee! this is the best news yet," cried Jack, with satisfaction.

"You've said it!" came from the twins; and Fred's face also showed his satisfaction.

"Well, we've certainly had a wonderful outing," declared Randy.

"And how many queer things have happened!" added his twin. "I don't believe we'll ever have as much excitement as this again."

But in this surmise Andy was mistaken. There were many happenings still in store for the boys, and what some of them were will be related in our next volume, to be entitled "The Rover Boys in the Land of Luck; Or, Stirring Adventures in the Oil Fields."

"Well, we'll be going back to Colby Hall before long," said Gif, that evening.

"But first you'll have to testify against those Germans and Tony Duval," answered Spouter.

"Good old Colby Hall!" cried Jack. "I don't know but what I'll be glad enough to get back there, after all, and see all the other fellows."

"And see the girls of Clearwater Hall, too," put in Andy slyly.

"We'll certainly have some stories to tell—how we brought down all that game," came from Fred, his eyes glistening.

Then in the best of good humor the boys started singing one of their favorite school songs. And here we will leave them and say good-bye.

THE END

Other books by this author

The Mystery at Putnam Hall

The Rover Boys at Colby Hall

The Rover Boys at College

The Rover Boys at School

The Rover Boys in New York

The Rover Boys in the Air

The Rover Boys in the Jungle

The Rover Boys In The Mountains

The Rover Boys on Land and Sea

The Rover Boys on the Great Lakes

The Rover Boys on the Ocean

The Rover Boys on the River

The Rover Boys out West

The Rover Boys on the Farm

Choose from Thousands of 1stWorldLibrary Classics By

A. M. Barnard	Booth Tarkington	Edward Everett Hale
Ada Leverson	Boyd Cable	Edward J. O'Biren
Adolphus William Ward	Bram Stoker	Edward S. Ellis
Aesop	C. Collodi	Edwin L. Arnold
Agatha Christie	C. E. Orr	Eleanor Atkins
Alexander Aaronsohn	C. M. Ingleby	Eleanor Hallowell Abbott
Alexander Kielland	Carolyn Wells	Eliot Gregory
Alexandre Dumas	Catherine Parr Traill	Elizabeth Gaskell
Alfred Gatty	Charles A. Eastman	Elizabeth McCracken
Alfred Ollivant	Charles Amory Beach	Elizabeth Von Arnim
Alice Duer Miller	Charles Dickens	Ellem Key
Alice Turner Curtis	Charles Dudley Warner	Emerson Hough
Alice Dunbar	Charles Farrar Browne	Emilie F. Carlen
Allen Chapman	Charles Ives	Emily Bronte
Alleyne Ireland	Charles Kingsley	Emily Dickinson
Ambrose Bierce	Charles Klein	Enid Bagnold
Amelia E. Barr	Charles Hanson Towne	Enilor Macartney Lane
Amory H. Bradford	Charles Lathrop Pack	Erasmus W. Jones
Andrew Lang	Charles Romyn Dake	Ernie Howard Pie
Andrew McFarland Davis	Charles Whibley	Ethel May Dell
Andy Adams	Charles Willing Beale	Ethel Turner
Angela Brazil	Charlotte M. Braeme	Ethel Watts Mumford
Anna Alice Chapin	Charlotte M. Yonge	Eugene Sue
Anna Sewell	Charlotte Perkins Stetson	Eugenie Foa
Annie Besant	Clair W. Hayes	Eugene Wood
Annie Hamilton Donnell	Clarence Day Jr.	Eustace Hale Ball
Annie Payson Call	Clarence E. Mulford	Evelyn Everett-green
Annie Roe Carr	Clemence Housman	Everard Cotes
Annonaymous	Confucius	F. H. Cheley
Anton Chekhov	Coningsby Dawson	F. J. Cross
Archibald Lee Fletcher	Cornelis DeWitt Wilcox	F. Marion Crawford
Arnold Bennett	Cyril Burleigh	Fannie E. Newberry
Arthur C. Benson	D. H. Lawrence	Federick Austin Ogg
Arthur Conan Doyle	Daniel Defoe	Ferdinand Ossendowski
Arthur M. Winfield	David Garnett	Fergus Hume
Arthur Ransome	Dinah Craik	Florence A. Kilpatrick
Arthur Schnitzler	Don Carlos Janes	Fremont B. Deering
Arthur Train	Donald Keyhoe	Francis Bacon
Atticus	Dorothy Kilner	Francis Darwin
B.H. Baden-Powell	Dougan Clark	Frances Hodgson Burnett
B. M. Bower	Douglas Fairbanks	Frances Parkinson Keyes
B. C. Chatterjee	E. Nesbit	Frank Gee Patchin
Baroness Emmuska Orczy	E. P. Roe	Frank Harris
Baroness Orczy	E. Phillips Oppenheim	Frank Jewett Mather
Basil King	E. S. Brooks	Frank L. Packard
Bayard Taylor	Earl Barnes	Frank V. Webster
Ben Macomber	Edgar Rice Burroughs	Frederic Stewart Isham
Bertha Muzzy Bower	Edith Van Dyne	Frederick Trevor Hill
Bjornstjerne Bjornson	Edith Wharton	Frederick Winslow Taylor

Friedrich Kerst
Friedrich Nietzsche
Fyodor Dostoyevsky
G.A. Henty
G.K. Chesterton
Gabrielle E. Jackson
Garrett P. Serviss
Gaston Leroux
George A. Warren
George Ade
Geroge Bernard Shaw
George Cary Eggleston
George Durston
George Ebers
George Eliot
George Gissing
George MacDonald
George Meredith
George Orwell
George Sylvester Viereck
George Tucker
George W. Cable
George Wharton James
Gertrude Atherton
Gordon Casserly
Grace E. King
Grace Gallatin
Grace Greenwood
Grant Allen
Guillermo A. Sherwell
Gulielma Zollinger
Gustav Flaubert
H. A. Cody
H. B. Irving
H. C. Bailey
H. G. Wells
H. H. Munro
H. Irving Hancock
H. R. Naylor
H. Rider Haggard
H. W. C. Davis
Haldeman Julius
Hall Caine
Hamilton Wright Mabie
Hans Christian Andersen
Harold Avery
Harold McGrath
Harriet Beecher Stowe
Harry Castlemon
Harry Coghill
Harry Houidini

Hayden Carruth
Helent Hunt Jackson
Helen Nicolay
Hendrik Conscience
Hendy David Thoreau
Henri Barbusse
Henrik Ibsen
Henry Adams
Henry Ford
Henry Frost
Henry James
Henry Jones Ford
Henry Seton Merriman
Henry W Longfellow
Herbert A. Giles
Herbert Carter
Herbert N. Casson
Herman Hesse
Hildegard G. Frey
Homer
Honore De Balzac
Horace B. Day
Horace Walpole
Horatio Alger Jr.
Howard Pyle
Howard R. Garis
Hugh Lofting
Hugh Walpole
Humphry Ward
Ian Maclaren
Inez Haynes Gillmore
Irving Bacheller
Isabel Cecilia Williams
Isabel Hornibrook
Israel Abrahams
Ivan Turgenev
J. G.Austin
J. Henri Fabre
J. M. Barrie
J. M. Walsh
J. Macdonald Oxley
J. R. Miller
J. S. Fletcher
J. S. Knowles
J. Storer Clouston
J. W. Duffield
Jack London
Jacob Abbott
James Allen
James Andrews
James Baldwin

James Branch Cabell
James DeMille
James Joyce
James Lane Allen
James Lane Allen
James Oliver Curwood
James Oppenheim
James Otis
James R. Driscoll
Jane Abbott
Jane Austen
Jane L. Stewart
Janet Aldridge
Jens Peter Jacobsen
Jerome K. Jerome
Jessie Graham Flower
John Buchan
John Burroughs
John Cournos
John F. Kennedy
John Gay
John Glasworthy
John Habberton
John Joy Bell
John Kendrick Bangs
John Milton
John Philip Sousa
John Taintor Foote
Jonas Lauritz Idemil Lie
Jonathan Swift
Joseph A. Altsheler
Joseph Carey
Joseph Conrad
Joseph E. Badger Jr
Joseph Hergesheimer
Joseph Jacobs
Jules Vernes
Julian Hawthrone
Julie A Lippmann
Justin Huntly McCarthy
Kakuzo Okakura
Karle Wilson Baker
Kate Chopin
Kenneth Grahame
Kenneth McGaffey
Kate Langley Bosher
Kate Langley Bosher
Katherine Cecil Thurston
Katherine Stokes
L. A. Abbot
L. T. Meade

L. Frank Baum
Latta Griswold
Laura Dent Crane
Laura Lee Hope
Laurence Housman
Lawrence Beasley
Leo Tolstoy
Leonid Andreyev
Lewis Carroll
Lewis Sperry Chafer
Lilian Bell
Lloyd Osbourne
Louis Hughes
Louis Joseph Vance
Louis Tracy
Louisa May Alcott
Lucy Fitch Perkins
Lucy Maud Montgomery
Luther Benson
Lydia Miller Middleton
Lyndon Orr
M. Corvus
M. H. Adams
Margaret E. Sangster
Margret Howth
Margaret Vandercook
Margaret W. Hungerford
Margret Penrose
Maria Edgeworth
Maria Thompson Daviess
Mariano Azuela
Marion Polk Angellotti
Mark Overton
Mark Twain
Mary Austin
Mary Catherine Crowley
Mary Cole
Mary Hastings Bradley
Mary Roberts Rinehart
Mary Rowlandson
M. Wollstonecraft Shelley
Maud Lindsay
Max Beerbohm
Myra Kelly
Nathaniel Hawthrone
Nicolo Machiavelli
O. F. Walton
Oscar Wilde
Owen Johnson
P.G. Wodehouse
Paul and Mabel Thorne

Paul G. Tomlinson
Paul Severing
Percy Brebner
Percy Keese Fitzhugh
Peter B. Kyne
Plato
Quincy Allen
R. Derby Holmes
R. L. Stevenson
R. S. Ball
Rabindranath Tagore
Rahul Alvares
Ralph Bonehill
Ralph Henry Barbour
Ralph Victor
Ralph Waldo Emmerson
Rene Descartes
Ray Cummings
Rex Beach
Rex E. Beach
Richard Harding Davis
Richard Jefferies
Richard Le Gallienne
Robert Barr
Robert Frost
Robert Gordon Anderson
Robert L. Drake
Robert Lansing
Robert Lynd
Robert Michael Ballantyne
Robert W. Chambers
Rosa Nouchette Carey
Rudyard Kipling
Saint Augustine
Samuel B. Allison
Samuel Hopkins Adams
Sarah Bernhardt
Sarah C. Hallowell
Selma Lagerlof
Sherwood Anderson
Sigmund Freud
Standish O'Grady
Stanley Weyman
Stella Benson
Stella M. Francis
Stephen Crane
Stewart Edward White
Stijn Streuvels
Swami Abhedananda
Swami Parmananda
T. S. Ackland

T. S. Arthur
The Princess Der Ling
Thomas A. Janvier
Thomas A Kempis
Thomas Anderton
Thomas Bailey Aldrich
Thomas Bulfinch
Thomas De Quincey
Thomas Dixon
Thomas H. Huxley
Thomas Hardy
Thomas More
Thornton W. Burgess
U. S. Grant
Upton Sinclair
Valentine Williams
Various Authors
Vaughan Kester
Victor Appleton
Victor G. Durham
Victoria Cross
Virginia Woolf
Wadsworth Camp
Walter Camp
Walter Scott
Washington Irving
Wilbur Lawton
Wilkie Collins
Willa Cather
Willard F. Baker
William Dean Howells
William le Queux
W. Makepeace Thackeray
William W. Walter
William Shakespeare
Winston Churchill
Yei Theodora Ozaki
Yogi Ramacharaka
Young E. Allison
Zane Grey